ANTHROPOLOGY AND/AS EDUCATION

There is more to education than teaching and learning, and more to anthropology than making studies of other people's lives. Here Tim Ingold argues that both anthropology and education are ways of studying, and of leading life, *with* others. In this provocative book, he goes beyond an exploration of the interface between the disciplines of anthropology and education to claim their fundamental equivalence.

Taking inspiration from the writings of John Dewey, Ingold presents his argument in four close-knit chapters. Education, he contends, is not the transmission of authorised knowledge from one generation to the next but a way of attending to things, opening up paths of growth and discovery. What does this mean for the ways we think about study and the school, teaching and learning, and the freedoms they exemplify? And how does it bear on the practices of participation and observation, on ways of study in the field and in the school, on art and science, research and teaching, and the university?

Written in an engaging and accessible style, this book is intended as much for educationalists as for anthropologists. It will appeal to all who are seeking alternatives to mainstream agendas in social and educational policy, including educators and students in philosophy, the social sciences, educational psychology, environmentalism and arts practice.

Tim Ingold is Professor of Social Anthropology at the University of Aberdeen, UK. His books for Routledge include *Lines* (2007), *Evolution and Social Life* (reissued 2016), *The Perception of the Environment* (reissued 2011), *Being Alive* (2011), *Making* (2013), and *The Life of Lines* (2015).

ANTHROPOLOGY AND/AS EDUCATION

Tim Ingold

LONDON AND NEW YORK

First published 2018
by Routledge
2 Park Square, Milton Park, Abingdon, Oxon OX14 4RN

and by Routledge
711 Third Avenue, New York, NY 10017

Routledge is an imprint of the Taylor & Francis Group, an informa business

© 2018 Tim Ingold

The right of Tim Ingold to be identified as author of this work has been asserted by him in accordance with sections 77 and 78 of the Copyright, Designs and Patents Act 1988.

British Library Cataloguing-in-Publication Data
A catalogue record for this book is available from the British Library

Library of Congress Cataloging-in-Publication Data
A catalog record for this book has been requested

ISBN: 978-0-415-78654-6 (hbk)
ISBN: 978-0-415-78655-3 (pbk)
ISBN: 978-1-315-22719-1 (ebk)

Typeset in Bembo
by Apex CoVantage, LLC

To the next generation
So that you may begin anew

CONTENTS

PREFACE AND ACKNOWLEDGEMENTS

For fifty years I have studied anthropology; for forty years I have taught it. Yet the idea that anthropology is not just a subject to be taught and studied, but educational in its very constitution, has crept up on me only over the last decade or so. Its source lay in a growing recognition of how much I had gained from working with students. It began to dawn on me that the classroom is far more than a place of instruction, wherein students could be introduced to the riches of what my colleagues like to call 'anthropological knowledge'. For this is to suppose that the work is already done, laid up in a literature amassed from the masterly contributions of illustrious forbears whose names we are supposed to learn and whose words we quote. It now seems to me, to the contrary, that the classroom is a place where much of the real anthropological work is carried on, a site of creative transformation in which we join with the thinking of our predecessors in order to go further, beyond what they would ever have imagined. The more convinced I was, however, of the educational value of the work that I and my fellow students were undertaking together, the more it seemed to contravene the requirements of teaching and learning set out in the institutional protocols to which we were expected to conform. According to these protocols, teaching is the delivery of content, learning its assimilation. But education, it seemed to me, is so much more than that. It is not, I contend, about the transmission of knowledge, but first and foremost about *leading life*. For me, the key moment came with the realisation that only once emancipated from the shackles of teaching and learning would our work in the classroom become truly educational.

The book before you is a result of this realisation. I want to prove that anthropological study, as a way of leading life with others, is educational through-and-through. This means venturing beyond an exploration of the interface between the disciplines of anthropology and education to argue for their more fundamental congruence. My claim, in short, is that the principles of anthropology are also the principles of education. To establish this claim, however, it is necessary to reassess these principles, on both sides.

On the side of education, this is a matter of overthrowing the traditional view of pedagogy as the inter-generational transmission of authorised knowledge. Education, I argue, is not a 'stilling in' but a 'leading out', which opens paths of intellectual growth and discovery without predetermined outcomes or fixed end-points. It is about attending to things, rather than acquiring the knowledge that absolves us of the need to do so; about exposure rather than immunisation. The task of the educator, then, is not to explicate knowledge for the benefit of those who are assumed, by default, to be ignorant, but to provide inspiration, guidance and criticism in the exemplary pursuit of truth. On the side of anthropology, my approach runs counter to the commonplace identification of anthropology with ethnography – to the assumption that what anthropologists do is study other peoples and their worlds. What makes anthropology educational rather than ethnographic, I contend, is that we don't so much study others as study *with* them. And having studied with others – or even while doing so – others come to study *with* us. The education we have undergone, in the first place, requires that we, in turn, become educators in the second. Though we might call the first 'the field' and the second 'the school', they are both places of study, and neither can exist without the other. That is why we must repudiate, once and for all, the belief that what goes on in the classroom, under the rubric of teaching and learning, is but auxiliary to an anthropological project whose primary objective is ethnographic. So long as anthropology and education remain on opposite sides of a division between the production of knowledge and its transmission, then in their effects they will forever cancel each other out. For pedagogy merely restores to actuality what ethnography has already extracted from it, albeit shorn of life's creative potential. By joining forces, however, and by recognising their common purpose, anthropology and education have the power to transform the world.

The immediate stimulus for writing this book came out of the blue, in the form of an invitation to present the 2016 Dewey Lectures to the Research Centre for Education, Learning and Didactics at the University of Rennes, France, in February 2016. I was honoured and delighted to receive this invitation, which could not have come at a more opportune moment, just as the idea of anthropology as education was beginning to stir in my mind. The lectures provided the perfect excuse for me to work the idea out, and to test it on an eager, sympathetic and yet critical audience. There were four lectures, respectively entitled 'Education is not knowledge transfer', 'Education and attention', 'Education in the minor key', and 'Education as correspondence'. As usual, the time I thought I would have to prepare them failed to materialise, and what I presented amounted to little more than rough notes, hurriedly put together. It would be no exaggeration to admit that to a large extent, I improvised as I went along. However with the lectures behind me, I was all fired up to write the book, and a respite from other tasks, in the summer months of 2016, eventually allowed me to make a start on it. By mid-August I was more than halfway through. Once again, however, other commitments intervened, and

I could not pick it up again until the run-up to Christmas. By mid-January 2017, I had a draft of the whole thing. In planning the book, I decided to stay close to the original lecture format: thus each chapter corresponds to a lecture, and even though (with one exception) their titles have changed and their contents developed beyond recognition, they nevertheless follow one another in the order presented.

One thread that runs through all four chapters is the educational philosophy of John Dewey. The opportunity to deliver a series of lectures in Dewey's name was not only a privilege, it also provided me with the incentive I needed to fulfil a long-held wish to better acquaint myself with his extensive writings. Reading the work of one of the leading public intellectuals of the early twentieth century, I was astonished by its prescience, by its clarity of expression, and by its conviction in spelling out principles that are as compelling today as they were a century ago. It remains a mystery to me that Dewey is so little known and so rarely acknowledged in anthropological circles. Even among philosophers, it seems, he has been largely forgotten. Yet turning on the wheel of rediscovery, we find ourselves retracing the roads he already mapped out for us. How much trouble we could have saved ourselves, had we joined his company from the start! Indeed with this book I offer my personal tribute to the great philosopher and educationalist, and an apology, albeit posthumously, for coming so late to his oeuvre.

But if the opportunity to deliver the Dewey Lectures provided the stimulus, the ideas I develop in this book have welled up principally from two other sources. The first is a five-year project, funded by the European Research Council, entitled *Knowing from the Inside: Anthropology, Art, Architecture and Design*, or KFI for short. The key ambition of the project is to reconfigure the relation between practices of inquiry and the knowledge to which they give rise, by developing and trialling a range of procedures that allow knowledge to grow from direct, practical and observational engagements with the people and things around us. This way of knowing – by studying *with* things or people instead of making studies *of* them – is, we suggest, the common thread that links anthropology to arts practice, and to the disciplines of architecture and design. By bringing these four disciplines together, we have sought to customise this general approach to knowing to specific fields of practice, and to contribute to both education and design for sustainable living through a renewed emphasis on the improvisational creativity and perceptual acuity of practitioners. The project commenced in 2013, and though still underway, one of its most important achievements so far has been to highlight the implications of our approach for the theory and practice of education. It has also led us to a way of doing anthropology with art, architecture and design that is more experimental and speculative than ethnographic. In May 2016, in the beautiful surroundings of Comrie, Perthshire, we put this approach to the test in a week-long programme of discussions, interventions and experiments. We called it *The KFI Kitchen*. Many of the ideas cooked up in the Kitchen have found their way into this book.

The second source of ideas for this book is very different. In October 2015, I initiated a campaign – under the banner 'Reclaiming our University' – to revitalise the institution in which I work, the University of Aberdeen, as a genuine community of students and scholars. There was a feeling at the time that the sense of community, which had always been one of the university's greatest strengths, was under threat from a regime of management that seemed bent on putting corporate interests before democratic responsibility. The idea was to get everyone across the institution talking about the kind of university we want, how it should be run, and how to achieve it. We did this through a series of open seminars, well-attended by both staff and students at all levels, on what emerged as the 'four pillars' of the coming university: *freedom*, *trust*, *education* and *community*. It was not enough, we realised, to appeal to these keywords as if they spoke for themselves. In order to develop a coherent vision, we needed to think in depth, and collectively, about what they really meant for us. The concept of 'academic freedom', for example, has been horribly abused by those who would appropriate and defend it as the exclusive entitlement of a scholarly elite. What kind of freedom, we had to ask ourselves, do we really want for our university? And again, what do we mean by 'education' when we speak of 'higher education', or of the inseparability of teaching and research? And what makes a 'community' out of the medley of often discordant voices and disciplines that are comprised by the university? Our discussions were passionate, constructive and – for me – transformative. We had already decided to condense the results into a manifesto, and over the summer of 2016, I struggled to draft its clauses. On 25 November, 2016, we launched our manifesto in the highly symbolic setting of the university's King's College Chapel. Much of what we say there has found its way into the following pages.

Many individuals have helped me write this book. First and foremost, I thank Gérard Sensevy for inviting me to present the Dewey Lectures at Rennes, and his colleagues and students for their responses and suggestions. Without their impetus, the book would never have been written. I also owe an enormous debt of gratitude to all who have participated, at one time or another, in the KFI project. There are too many to name, and I could not single out some while omitting others. So with these words I send my thanks to all: you know who you are! In addition, I am extremely grateful to the European Research Council for the funding that has made the project possible through the award of an Advanced Grant (323677 – KFI). Back in Aberdeen, I am especially indebted to all the 'reclaimers' who have joined with me in our campaign to restore the university to its rightful community. Though I would not wish to cause embarrassment by naming them, you too know who you are, and I thank you all. However I do want to name three scholars who, through their presence and publications, have had a powerful impact on my thinking, and on this work. They are Jan Masschelein, Gert Biesta and Erin Manning. I want to thank them for their inspiration. Finally, I dedicate this book to coming generations, including those of my own lineage, the latest of whom – Leo Arthur Raphaely-Ingold – arrived as this work was in progress. They are our future, and I wish them well.

Tim Ingold
Aberdeen, February 2017

1

AGAINST TRANSMISSION

Leaving school

For those of us raised in nominally western or modern societies, the word 'education' most commonly summons up memories of going to school. We went there, so we recall, to be educated: to learn to read and write, to count and calculate, and by these means to become conversant with all the branches of knowledge, from the sciences to the arts and letters, that make up the legacy of our civilisation. Of our children, we might perhaps acknowledge that their education commences even before they go to school, in those pre-school institutions, traditionally known as nurseries and kindergartens, where the seeds of future learning are planted. And we might ourselves have benefited from education even after leaving school, by attending institutions going by a variety of names – colleges, universities, polytechnics – which claim to take us either 'further' or 'higher', depending on their academic status, along the road to civility. But the school, in our usual reckoning, remains the primary site of educational formation, in relation to which pre-school is understood as preparation and post-school as fulfilment. In a democratically constituted society, it is of course the responsibility of the state to ensure adequate educational provision for its citizens, and the minister of state for education is tasked, above all, with the oversight of schools, and with the regulation of what goes on in them, including what gets taught and how.

The practice of education and the institution of the school, in short, seem joined at the hip. You cannot apparently have one without the other. What are we to say, then, of societies without schools, or where only a minority enjoy the privilege of attending them? Is it acceptable to say of persons who have not been to school that they are uneducated, and therefore uncivilised? Such persons know a great deal that we, educated folk, do not. Anthropologists have gone to great lengths to document this knowledge, to reveal its detail, sophistication and accuracy, and to uncover the processes by which it is acquired. They have denounced, with good reason, the division of the peoples of the world into educated and uneducated, civilised and primitive. This is no more than a reflection, they say, of ethnocentric prejudice. Knowledge differs from culture to culture, as do the institutions that facilitate its passage from each generation to the next. The school is one such institution, but there are plenty of others. Is education, then, something that happens to every human being, living in society, as they pass from immaturity to maturity? Might it perhaps be listed alongside those capacities, including for language and symbolic thought, which are often considered to be the distinguishing marks of humanity? All animals learn, of course, in the sense of adjusting their ways of doing things in response to prevailing environmental conditions. It is quite another matter, however, to set up virtual scenarios in anticipation of conditions not currently prevalent but that might plausibly be encountered at some time in the future, so as to instruct novices in how to deal with them. Deliberate instruction of this kind – or what is generally known as pedagogy – may indeed be uniquely human.[1]

Pedagogy is the art of teaching. There are all sorts of ways of distinguishing between teaching and learning, or of showing how the one exceeds the other, depending for example on whether the learner merely picks up habits from observations of what others do or has them deliberately demonstrated, or on whether the demonstration is framed in terms of rules or principles abstracted from contexts of application. Learning to make a flaked stone tool in the presence of a master knapper exemplifies the former; learning to navigate by means of star charts exemplifies the latter.[2] These distinctions, of great significance to students of comparative human and non-human behaviour, are not of immediate concern to me at this point. What does concern me is an assumption that runs through virtually all discussion of these matters, namely that education in its broadest sense is about the *transmission of information*.[3] For those who hold that education takes place in schools, the school is taken to be a sequestered space in which knowledge is transmitted, in advance of its application when students take it out into the world beyond. For those who hold that education is a practice of pedagogy universal to humans, whether they attend school or not, the same logic applies. The school may not be the only kind of institution vested with a pedagogic purpose, but alternative institutional practices ranging from storytelling to ritual initiation may still be modelled on it, at least in analysis, and credited with an equivalent function. Thus they may be said to operate in a 'school-like' way, to transmit the legacy of custom, morality and belief that adds up to what we call a 'culture' to each successive generation, such that it may subsequently be expressed and enacted in the practice of everyday life.

My aim in this chapter is to argue against the idea of transmission, to show that this is not the way in which people ordinarily come to know what they do, that indeed it seriously distorts the purpose and meaning of education. This, in turn, will lay the foundation for my next chapter, in which I shall argue that education is really about attending to things, and to the world. In short, I want to prove that education is a practice of attention, not of transmission – that it is through attention that knowledge is both generated and carried on. To make the case against transmission, I begin with the writings of John Dewey, pragmatist and philosopher, justly regarded as the pre-eminent educational theorist of the early twentieth century, whose book *Democracy and Education* was published exactly a century ago.[4]

The continuity of life

Who would have thought of opening a treatise on education with the following sentence: 'The most notable distinction between living and inanimate things is that the former maintain themselves by renewal'?[5] Dewey's point of departure is not the school, nor the people, nor even humanity. Rather than starting from the idea of education as schooling and then extending out to wider domains of human and even non-human culture, Dewey proceeds in quite the opposite direction. To understand what education is about, he says, the first thing to which we have to attend is the nature of life. We have to understand how plants and animals differ from stones. The stone, beaten by the elements, wears away or even breaks apart. But living things, quite to the contrary, take in the elemental energies and substances – light, moisture and earth – and turn them into a force for their own growth and self-renewal. Yet they cannot keep this up indefinitely, nor can they proceed in isolation. Every life is tasked with bringing other lives into being and with sustaining them for however long it takes for the latter, in turn, to engender further life. The continuity of the life process is therefore not individual but social. And education in its broadest sense, according to Dewey, is 'the means of this social continuity of life'.[6] Wherever and whenever life is going on, so too is education. It is going on, more narrowly, in spheres of *human* life and in the latter, most particularly, in the *school*.

Yet the school, far from realising the educational imperative in its purest form, is but one of many means for securing social continuity, and a relatively superficial one at that, prone to the distortion that comes from isolating the informational content of knowledge from the life-experience through which, and only through which, it can take on any kind of meaning. Indeed education in the sense Dewey intended is more likely to be going on beyond the school than within its walls. What is truly essential to education, for Dewey, is not formal pedagogy, mediated through such specialised cognitive instruments as language and symbolic representation, but *transmission* and *communication*. These are not just means that make it possible for social life to go on; they are of the essence of social life itself. 'Society', says Dewey, 'not only continues to exist *by* transmission, *by* communication, but it may fairly be said to exist *in* transmission, *in* communication'.[7] Now at first glance, this assertion seems to fly in the face of my own ambition for this chapter, which is precisely to argue *against* the idea of education as a process of transmission, and by implication of communication. I aim to show that transmission is the death of education, and that it takes the very heart out of social life. How, then, can I possibly adduce Dewey in my support? To answer this question, we need to take a closer look at the meanings of these key terms, communication and transmission. For the senses in which Dewey employs them are not at all the same as those in common use today, inflected as they have been by the revolutions in informatics and communications technology that dominated the second half of the twentieth century.

Let me start with 'communication'. For most of us today, this has to do with conveying information, or sending messages. I have something to impart: I encode it in some physical form that allows it to be conveyed to you with minimal distortion; you receive the package and decode the contents. Ideally, you should then end up in possession of exactly the same information as I began with. You may, in return, send something back; we could then speak of communication as the *exchange* of information. But this is not how Dewey understands the term. Noting the affinity between the words, 'communication', 'community' and 'common', he is interested in how people with different experiences of life can reach an accord – a degree of like-mindedness that allows them to carry on their lives together.[8] Perhaps, following medieval precedent, one could turn 'common' into a verb; to communicate would then be 'to common'.[9] In contexts of education, this commoning is above all an achievement of persons of different generations. Its educative power, furthermore, lies in the fact that information does *not* pass from head to head without distortion. For if I am to share my experience with you, it is not enough to package and send it as it is. You might receive the package, but will be none the wiser for it. For sharing to be educative, I have to make an imaginative effort to cast my experience in ways that can join with yours, so that we can – in a sense – travel the same paths and, in so doing, make meaning together.[10] It is not that you end with a piece of knowledge implanted in your mind that once had belonged only to me; rather we come into a concordance that is new to both of us. Education is transformative.

Commoning and variation

Now what education is to the continuity of life, in Dewey's usage, communication is to transmission. The one is the means to the other. Though Dewey takes less care to define 'transmission' than he does 'communication', it is clear that the one thing he does *not* mean by the term is what it is conventionally taken to mean nowadays, namely the conveyance, from one generation to the next, of a corpus of instructions and representations for the conduct of a form of life. Transmission is possible, Dewey argues, because lives overlap, because as some grow older and eventually die, others are already born and growing up. It is through participation in each other's lives – through the ongoing and unrelenting efforts of young and old, immature and mature, to reach a concordance of sorts – that education proceeds and the knowledge, values, beliefs and practices of a society are perpetuated. Indeed Dewey is insistent that only if there is participation on both sides can education be carried on. Senior and junior parties must share a stake in the outcome. If they do not, then what we have is not education but what Dewey calls 'training'. You can train a domestic animal to behave in the way you want by rewarding it, for example, with morsels of food. But so long as the animal's interest is in the food, not in the service rendered to its master, then this does not amount to education. All too often, Dewey laments, the young of our own kind are similarly treated, the child 'trained like an animal rather than educated like a human being'.[11] Insofar as such training moulds the raw material of immature humans to a pre-existent design, while it might replicate the design, it serves no educational purpose whatsoever.

This is the moment to introduce a third term which, alongside communication and transmission, plays a key role in Dewey's philosophy of education. This is 'environment'. As communication is the commoning of life and transmission its perpetuation, so environment is its variation. That is to say, it is not simply what surrounds the individual, or the sum total of encompassing conditions. What makes an environment is the way in which these conditions are drawn, over time, into a pattern of conjoint activity. Imagine an astronomer, gazing at the stars. For him the stars, however remote, are part of the environment – they are of *concern* to him. And being of concern, they cause him to vary as his gaze wanders from star to star. Reasoning from this example, Dewey concludes that 'the things with which a man varies are his genuine environment'.[12] They go along with him, and vary as he does, in accordance with his inclinations and dispositions. One way of putting this is in terms of question and answer. The stars question the astronomer, they arouse his curiosity, and he is moved to respond. This response is not just a reaction, as if to a disturbance of vision that irrupts into consciousness, but an answering that prolongs the astronomer's own tendency, which lies in the desire to know them better. We might say, as indeed Dewey does, that the astronomer *corresponds* with the stars. The promise of education lies in the capacity to respond and to be responded to: without such 'response ability', as we might call it, education would be impossible.[13] The idea of response ability is key to my argument in this book, and is one to which I shall return. For the present, I would like to conclude this section by establishing the link between communication as commoning and environment as variation.

The point I want to emphasise is that there is no contradiction, as might appear at first glance, between these two terms. Rather, commoning and variation are co-dependent. On the one hand, there can be no movement, growth or life in the sharing of experience unless there is variation in what each participant brings into it. The achievement of commonality is not the discovery of what individuals have in common to begin with: it is a continual creation, not a regress to an origin. In the absence of variation, the only difference could be between those with more endowments and those with less, and education – as a direct transfer of knowledge and values from the former to the latter – would be reduced to training. As Dewey is at pains to stress, immaturity is not a lack, it is a specific power of growth, and the purpose of education is not to fill a void in the mind of the child so as to raise it to the level of the adult, but to bring young and old together in order that social life should carry on. Even as the young grow old, in sharing in the wisdom born of long experience, so the old grow young in sharing the sympathetic curiosity, sensitivity and openness of mind of their juniors.[14] There is no end to it: growth can only be a means to further growth as is life to further life. On the other hand, there can be no variation without co-participation in a shared social environment. It is in the correspondence with others – in answering to them, not in the receipt of what is handed down – that each of us comes into our own as a person with a singular and recognisable voice. Whereas training suppresses difference, or admits it only on the margins as idiosyncrasy, education fosters difference as the very fount of personhood.

To sum up: commoning and variation depend on one another, and both are necessary for the continuity of life. The educational community is held together through variation, not by similarity. It is a community – not just a living together but literally a *giving* together (from *com-*, 'together', plus *-munus*, 'gift') – in which everyone has something to give precisely because they have nothing in common, and in which generous co-existence overcomes the essentialist regression to a primordial identity.[15] 'Having in common' – like humanity itself – is not a baseline but an aspiration; not given from the start but a task that calls for communal effort. This effort demands of everyone, young and old, that they open up to others, each contributing, in his or her own actions, to the conditions of common life from which further variation arises. Thus do the people of each generation play their part in establishing the environmental conditions under which their successors are raised and grow to maturity. And Dewey's conclusion, on these grounds, is that education cannot take place by 'direct conveyance' but only indirectly, 'through the intermediary of the environment'.[16] But in the age of informatics, it is precisely to direct conveyance, and *not* to the continuity of life-in-an-environment, that the concept of transmission has come to refer. That is why, in the name of Dewey, I now take up arms against it.

The genealogical model

Consider the relation between parent and child. The former may be mother or father; the latter a son or daughter. In anthropological parlance, the technical term for the relation, irrespective of gender, is *filiation*. How, then, should we describe it? On the kinship charts of anthropologists, it has long been conventional to depict filiation as a vertical line connecting two diamond-shaped icons. The icons stand for persons, their diamond shape signifying that they may be male or female. But what is the significance of the line? It only takes a second glance to realise that this apparently innocent depiction is bristling with hidden assumptions. The first is that in the relation of filiation, the lives of parent and child are not joined but kept well apart. They are separated from the outset, and ever remain so, no more, no less. Far from reaching out or responding to one another, they remain confined to their respective places, each inside their particular icon. Ageing neither removes the parent further from the child, nor brings her closer; growth and maturation bring the child no closer to the parent. In the second place the line is not, therefore, a line of life. Whatever it conducts is not life itself but a set of endowments, properties or instructions for living it. And third, since the line is there from the off, and does not grow or extend over time, these attributes must be endowed independently and in advance of the child's growth and development in the world. According to the chart, in short, filiation is direct, and wholly unmediated by environmental experience. And the line? It is, of course, a line of transmission. Along such lines, individuals come into immediate possession of attributes (properties, endowments, characteristics) that already exist, prior to putting them into play in the business of life. Or in a word, they *inherit*.

Evidently the kinship chart applies a determinate logic. It is the logic of what I have called the *genealogical model*, the defining assumption of which is that individuals are specified in their essential constitution, independently and in advance of their life in the world, through the bestowal of attributes from ancestors.[17] To forestall any possible misunderstanding, I do not for one moment mean to suggest that the many peoples around the world who like to record and recite their genealogies have resort to this logic.[18] Far from it! In the stories they tell of their illustrious ancestors, of begetting and being begotten, every generation leans over and touches the next, like fibres that – aligned longitudinally – secure the continuity of the whole rope that reaches from past to present.[19] These are life stories. The genealogical model, by contrast, is an artefact of formal anthropological analysis, the origination of which is often credited to one of anthropology's own more illustrious ancestors, W. H. R. Rivers. Indeed the method that Rivers proposed, in the early decades of the twentieth century, for the rigorous collection and analysis of genealogical data remains in common use today.[20] However the model is by no means exclusive to anthropology, and it could be that Rivers's achievement was more strictly to have customised, for the study of human kinship, a way of thinking that was already well established, at least across the sciences of biology and psychology. It is true that in recent anthropology the model has been subjected to sustained critique, partly in the light of the insistence – among those with whom anthropologists have worked – that relations of kinship are not predetermined by genetic connection but forged as people live together, often under one roof, and contribute materially and experientially to each other's formation.[21] In biology and psychology, however, the genealogical model remains alive and well, and for the most part unquestioned.

In biology, the model underwrites the twin distinctions between genotype and phenotype, and between phylogeny and ontogeny. Whereas the genotype is supposed to furnish a formal design specification of the organism-to-be, given at the point of conception and coded in the genome, the phenotype is the manifest form that arises from the organism's growth and maturation in a specific environment. A fundamental premise of the model, originally enunciated by August Weismann at the close of the nineteenth century (though in terms that predated the language of modern genetics), is that only the elements of the genotype, and not those of the phenotype, can be passed across generations in an ancestor-descendant sequence. Thus the expression of these elements is confined within each generation to the life cycle of the individual. It follows that just as filiation is orthogonal to growth and maturation in the anthropology of persons, so descent is orthogonal to life, or phylogeny to ontogeny, in the biology of organisms. In psychology the same logic is played out in the classic distinction between social and individual learning: the first referring to the way in which context-free information, specifying the patterns of cultural life, is copied across from tutor to novice, the second to novices' repeated attempts to apply already copied information within particular environmental contexts of action. Indeed, so perfect is the logical compatibility between biological and psychological versions of the genealogical model that scholars have been quick to propose synthetic theories of biocultural evolution according to which genetic and cultural information passes down parallel tracks. Every individual is said to inherit two sets of specifications, one established through genetic replication, the other through the replication – by way of observation and imitation – of analogous units of culture, which are together brought to bear in subsequent interaction with the environment.[22]

The fixation in these theories on the concept of inheritance is the surest indication that the genealogical model is at work. The model is however disabled by a fallacy that lies at its very core. Succinctly expressed by the philosopher of biology Susan Oyama, it is that information must be presumed to 'pre-exist the processes that give rise to it'.[23] The fallacy is as disabling for the idea of genetic transmission as it is for its cultural analogue. I begin with the former, before turning to the latter, with which I am principally concerned.

Undoing the circle

The genome of an organism, present in every cell of the body, is made up of long lengths of deoxyribonucleic acid (DNA) which have the singular property, within the chemical matrix of the cell, of turning out copies with identical sequences of acidic bases. This property, remarkable in itself, is not however so remarkable as to warrant the conclusion that the DNA sequence already encodes a character specification for the organism. The replication of the molecule is one thing, the reproduction of the organism quite another, and a link between them can only be established by way of the process of ontogenetic development – that is of the organism's growth and maturation within a specific environment. The idea of the 'genetic trait' is therefore a contradiction in terms insofar as it attributes, to what is copied at the inauguration of the life-cycle, properties that only emerge in the course of development. In the genotype, conceived (in contradistinction to the molecular genome) as a complex of traits, the organism appears to be completed even before it is begun, its life-cycle collapsed into an iconic point – precisely as in the kinship charts of anthropologists. Indeed the genotype, in truth, is no more than a formal, context-independent description of the organism, shorn of environmentally induced variation. As such, it exists nowhere save in the imagination of the observing biologist who, having installed it at the heart of the organism as a programme or blueprint for subsequent development – that is, as a *bio-logos* – sees the organism's unfolding life merely as a transcription, under specific environmental conditions, of what has been inscribed at the start.[24]

The circularity of this reasoning needs no further comment. I draw attention to it only because an equivalent circularity arises whenever the genealogical model is applied, by analogy, to learned tradition. For the copying of genetic traits, the model substitutes the copying of analogous traits of culture. And what replication does for genes, imitation is said to do for culture. Whether unique to humans or not, cultural inheritance is supposed to rest on an instinct to imitate, which automatically causes overt behaviour, witnessed by the observant neophyte, to be imprinted in the neophyte's mind as a covert schema for its replication. However, this appeal to the imitative instinct, as Dewey pointed out a century ago, mistakes the like-mindedness that results from living together for a psychological force that produces it. It is, he caustically observed, to put the cart before the horse: 'it takes an effect for the cause of the effect'.[25] Quite so! Indeed the idea of the 'cultural trait' is as much a contradiction in terms as its genetic counterpart, and for the same reason: it begins where it ends. What is sometimes called the 'culture-type', by analogy with the genotype, installs at the outset – as a complex of traits – habits or dispositions that can only arise through conjoint practice and experience in an environment.[26] Like the genotype, the culture-type is a descriptive formalisation of observed behaviour which the analyst imagines to be copied *in* to the minds of the individuals of a culture only to find that it is copied *out* in their subsequent (and consequent) behaviour. That the learning entailed in copying should be called 'social', although it is alleged to precede the recipient's entry into the theatre of social life, and that the learning which follows should be called 'individual' even though it is performed with others in this very theatre, only highlights the confusion. Theorists of cultural inheritance, it seems, have contrived to compress everything social into the heads of individuals, leaving the environment bereft of any social relationality whatever and invoked for no other reason than that individuals should have something tangible to interact with.

All this is not, of course, to deny that imitation or copying goes on among human beings, and possibly among animals of other kinds, or that it is necessary to secure intergenerational continuity. But it does not so much precede environmentally situated practice as proceed by way of it. As Dewey puts it, imitation is 'a misleading name for partaking with others in a use of things which leads to consequences of common interest'.[27] The problem, then, is how to transform experience in such a way that it can join in the production of commonality. How can 'the young assimilate the point of view of the old', Dewey asks, or 'the older bring the young into like-mindedness with themselves?' His answer, in its most general formulation, is 'by means of the action of the environment in calling out certain responses'. As the environment undergoes continuous variation, so the person varies in answer to it, and vice versa. The old, in their manner or comportment, vary with the young; the young, in their endeavours to reproduce what they observe, vary with the old. Or in short, what we are inclined to call imitation is really a modality of correspondence. But if that is so, then by the same token it cannot be understood as a modality of transmission – not, at least, in the sense of transmission implied by the genealogical model. It is simply impossible, Dewey insists, for the beliefs and attitudes that a social group cultivates in its immature members to be 'hammered in' or 'plastered on'; they cannot be 'physically extracted and inserted', and they cannot spread by 'direct contagion' or 'literal inculcation'. You might be able to do such things with material entities like nails, teeth and germs, but not with ideas whose very formation depends on experience.[28]

Whatever the force of Dewey's strictures, they appear to have had little impact on mainstream psychology, whose practitioners continue to think that elements of mental content such as beliefs and attitudes can be extracted and inserted in just the way that he so strenuously sought to refute, and have devoted much effort to the discovery of built-in cognitive mechanisms that would bring about this miraculous feat. Some psychologists, together with a handful of anthropological camp-followers, and rather more from biology, have even taken to calling these mental elements 'memes'. Just as genes inhabit the body and control its ontogenetic development, so memes – they claim – inhabit the mind and control the carrier's thought and behaviour. This is not, in fact, a new idea. Though popularised in the last decades by biologist Richard Dawkins and his acolytes, it has been present in the literature for a century or more, its longevity matched only by its proponents' unwavering conviction that it stands at the cutting edge of science.[29] Indeed it is hard to resist the conclusion, to which I shall return below, that the idea of memetic transmission is itself an inverted image of scientific rationality, as reflected in the mirror of culture. Perhaps that is why it has proved so tenacious, for so long.

How to follow a recipe

One recent anthropological advocate of the idea is Dan Sperber, though he calls the transmitted elements 'representations' in preference to 'memes'.[30] According to Sperber, representations are directly contagious: they can spread through a population like an epidemic, infecting minds primed by heredity to receive them and causing their hosts to behave in ways conducive to their further propagation – much as having caught a cold, you are inclined to sneeze. Thus the air is thick with information-bearing particles, which are picked up, spread about and replicated as we go about our everyday business. Among these particles – to cite one of Sperber's favourite examples – would formerly have been spoken sounds that encode instructions for the preparation of Mornay sauce. These sounds, once part of an oral culinary tradition, have nowadays been largely displaced by ink patterns visible on the pages of recipe books. Either way, the aspiring cook has only to decode the sounds or the patterns to receive the instructions, now implanted as representations in her mind. And to prepare the sauce, all she needs do is to convert these instructions into bodily behaviour, though the precise way in which this is done may of course depend on specific features of her kitchen.[31]

There is however a catch in this story, which lies in the conditions of encoding and decoding. If sounds or ink patterns are to serve as vectors for the transmission of instructions, and if these instructions are to be received in their entirety in advance of any actual cookery – for how else could they be 'converted into behaviour'? – then we must have some way of putting meaning into sounds and patterns, and of reading meaning from them, which is independent of any context of action. To restate the issue in more general terms: there can be no direct transmission of information from one context of enactment to another without rules of encoding and decoding that are themselves context-independent. The meanings of spoken or written words, or of any other symbols that might be used (such as numeric or geometric), must be given in advance. Once again, Dewey was already onto the problem long before his successors were even aware of it. Our familiarity with both spoken and written language, he notes, is such that we are easily deceived into thinking that knowledge can be inserted directly into the mind of another: 'it almost seems as if all we have to do … is to convey a sound into his ear'.[32] Merely whisper the words 'melt the butter in a pan and stir in the flour' and a Mornay sauce will magically materialise! But there is, as Dewey tells us, far more to it than that.

Assuming for a start that I speak your language (and thus putting in brackets the wealth of childhood experience by which we have come into possession of our mother tongue), I can follow what you say only because it corresponds to my experience, as it does to yours, of melting and stirring, of handling such substances as flour and butter, and of finding the relevant ingredients and utensils from the various corners of my kitchen. The verbal instructions of the recipe, in other words, draw their meanings neither from their attachment to mental representations inside my head, nor from their attachment to those inside yours, but from their positioning within the familiar environment of the home.[33] True, had I read the words in a recipe book rather than had them in my ear, I might never have met the author; indeed we may have lived far apart in space and time. But as Dewey observes, physical proximity does not in itself create community: 'a book or a letter may institute a more intimate association between human beings separated thousands of miles from each other than exists between dwellers under the same roof'.[34] What matters is that we have experience to share. And this was Dewey's point. Neither verbal sounds nor the graphic marks of writing, he insisted, come with their meanings already attached; rather they gather their meanings, in the same way that things do, from their enrolment in the shared experience of joint activity. Agreement on the meanings of words is an achievement of commoning: we have continually to work at it, and for that reason it is always provisional, never final.

The experience that you and I share, or that I share with the author of the recipe book, is of travelling through a field of associated tasks. Elsewhere I have coined the term 'taskscape' to refer to this field.[35] Like signposts in a landscape, the instructions in the book provide specific indications for practitioners as they make their way around the taskscape, each instruction strategically located at a point which the author, looking back on previous experience of preparing the dish in question, considered to be a critical juncture in the total process. Between these points, the cook is expected to be able to find his or her way, attentively and responsively, but without further recourse to explicit rules of procedure – or in a word, skilfully. In itself, then, the recipe is not knowledge. Rather, it opens up a path to knowledge, thanks to its location within a taskscape that is already partially familiar by virtue of previous experience. Only when placed in the context of skills gained through prior experience does information specify a route that is comprehensible and that can practicably be followed, and only a route so specified can lead to knowledge. It is in this sense that all knowledge is founded in skill. Just as my knowledge of the landscape is gained by walking through it, following various signposted routes, so my knowledge of cookery comes from following the several recipes of the book. This is not knowledge that has been transmitted *to* me; it is knowledge that has grown *in* me as I have followed the same paths as my predecessors and under their direction.[36]

Recipes, in this sense, are just like stories. They have a narrative structure: 'first do this, then that; observe, as you do this and that, how the consistency of your ingredients changes'. And everything I have said about recipes applies to stories too. Anthropologists have been right to draw attention to the educative functions of storytelling, the world over. But they have been wrong to conclude that stories are therefore vectors for the coded transmission of information that, once deciphered, would reveal a comprehensive system of knowledge, beliefs and values.[37] Far from coming with their meanings already attached, the significance of stories – just like the significance of instructions in the recipe book – is something that listeners have to find for themselves, by drawing them into correspondence with their own experience and life histories.[38] Stories overlap, with each telling leaning over and touching the next. So too do the lives of which they tell. That's the way they carry on. It is worth recalling, here, my earlier distinction between the genealogical model and the recitation of genealogies. One gives us a connected sequence of ancestors and descendants, in which every link between parent and child is a line of transmission. But the other gives us a correspondence of lives – now overlapping, now overtaken – commoning and varying as they go. As experienced rather than modelled, filiation is not a link in a chain but a 'growing older together' that continues until the parental life is cast off, by which time the child will have founded other lives with which to correspond.[39]

Reason and inheritance

In view of all the objections that have been raised against the notion of education as transmission or 'direct conveyance', and not only in the writings of Dewey, its obstinate persistence calls for some explanation. Dewey himself wondered why, despite widespread condemnation of the ideas of teaching as a kind of decanting, and of learning as passive absorption, they had nevertheless remained so entrenched in practice. For him it was a source of considerable frustration.[40] A century later, not much has changed. At school, students are still expected to follow a curriculum which has been laid down in advance, and to progress through measurable stages from initiation to completion. It seems as if some inexorable logic drives us to impose an ever more constrained and finite regime of pedagogic training, at the same time that we exalt the value of education as the royal road to rational enlightenment. I am reminded of the piano lessons I had to endure as a child. Through a mixture of threats and incentives, which had nothing to do with music, I was cajoled into practising scales and arpeggios. Devoid of melodic interest, they were to be played evenly and without expression. Only through undergoing such mechanically determined motions, I was told, could I have any hope of eventually achieving the virtuosity and expressive freedom exemplified by masters of the instrument. Needless to say, I abandoned this regime as soon as I could, and have derived much musical enjoyment from my uneven but nevertheless variable playing ever since. The contradictory appeal to freedom and determinism, here as in so many other fields of endeavour, flies in the face of Dewey's call for an education dedicated to the growth of persons in community. Could it be that the very ideal of enlightenment is what keeps the transmission model alive? The history of anthropology provides a clue to the answer.

To say that anthropology has long had a problem with the concept of culture would be an understatement. The problem lies in the fact that the very same word with which, among our own kind, we exalt the refinement of taste and manners is also routinely applied to the heritage of other, unlettered folk whose thought and conduct is supposed to follow the dictates of tradition.[41] Historically, anthropology has lurched from one extreme to the other, from the celebrated definition of 'Culture or Civilisation' with which Edward Burnett Tylor opened his *Primitive Culture* of 1871, encompassing everything 'acquired by man as a member of society', to Robert Lowie's ostensible borrowing of the same definition in his *History of Ethnological Theory* of 1937, where culture nevertheless became 'the sum total of what an individual acquires from his society … not by his own creative efforts but as a legacy from the past'.[42] For Tylor, Culture (always in the singular and with a capital 'C') was the great civilisational process by which humanity had progressively lifted itself up, to different degrees among different nations, from rude superstition to reason and enlightenment. Lowie, on the contrary, saw in culture an almost haphazard diversity of habitual ways of living and thinking, effortlessly absorbed by its myriad carriers. For the entirety of human culture, which Tylor had called a 'complex whole', Lowie famously substituted a 'planless hodgepodge'.[43] The difference between their respective definitions hinged on what it means to say that culture is 'acquired'. Tylor's 'man in society', in pursuing his own advancement, actively acquires knowledge through intellectual inquiry. Lowie's 'individual', on the other hand, effortlessly soaks up whatever he is exposed to, acquiring his culture as an already completed inheritance. Arguably, however, it was the very project of Culture that precipitated the perceived inertia of cultural tradition. 'Man in society', having reached the summit and surveying the landscape of humanity from his Olympian heights, sees only the 'hodgepodge' beneath, of individuals caught in their diverse ways, trapped by the legacies of the past and lacking the creative energy to break out. We *have* Culture and they do not because they are *had by* culture and we are not.

Today we see this same duplicity in debates over 'science' and 'traditional knowledge'. Thanks to the combined efforts of anthropologists and their consultants, it is now widely recognised that people who still inhabit the land and draw a living from it, yet who may have benefited little from 'western' education, know their environments in ways that are extensive, detailed and precise. Their knowledge grows and is grown in the correspondence not only of successive generations but also with animals, plants and the land. Even scientists, who had formerly dismissed the knowledge of inhabitants as too subjective, qualitative and anecdotal to be of value, have finally woken up to its potential significance. But what science still finds hard to grasp is the nature of this knowledge. For the project of science, conceived as the acquisition of knowledge through empirical inquiry and rational analysis, precipitates its opposite, namely knowledge that appeals to neither fact nor reason, but to the legacy of tradition. The result is that ways of knowing which are nothing if not dynamic and open-ended come to be recast in the scientific imagination as fixed formulae, handed down without question and with the authority of time immemorial. The people themselves, though it is conceded that they know, are not expected to know that they know. Nor do they realise how, unbeknownst to them – through countless generations of miscopying-in-transmission, accidents of recombination, and a sifting of alternatives depending on which are most successful in getting their carriers to behave in ways conducive to their further propagation – their knowledge has come to be so well adapted to life in the environments they inhabit. Culture adapts, declare the scientists (as though it were some great discovery rather than a reflection of their own reason), in ways analogous to adaptation by variation under natural selection in the organic domain! But the adaptive functions of so-called traditional knowledge, and the selective forces that have shaped it, are – according to this narrative – evident only to the scientists who framed it in the first place, not to the people who are apparently destined to expend their lives in its enactment.[44]

Traditional knowledge, in short, is an artefact of scientific reason, precipitated by science's own claim to have transcended it. Assimilated to the culture-type, it belongs to a rationalisation of behaviour precisely analogous to the equivalent genotypic rationalisation of organic design. Both genotype and culture-type, as we have already seen, are thrown up by the genealogical model, which substitutes for growth and development the binary of reason and inheritance. On one side of the binary are scientists and other people *of* Culture; on the other side are the custodians of traditional knowledge, people *in* culture. And if the latter, not knowing what they know, are to cross the Rubicon from tradition to reason, then paradoxically, they need science to re-educate them in their own knowledge, to explain it back to them in formal terms, so that they can see how it might be used as an instrument of rational management and in order to free them from the shackles of the past. The paradox is not however confined to the peculiar dialogue of science and traditional knowledge. It is found, too, in contemporary discourses of education, where the same Rubicon divides the naivety of childhood from adult intelligence. We are convinced that children should be educated in order that they can cross from one condition to the other. To this end, the world they know from experience has to be returned to them in rationalised form, as a system of rules and principles, or what once were called *rudiments*. Drained of environmental variation, these rudiments are conveyed to students as if they mapped an already known continent, serving as a territorial foundation for their own ascent to reason. The world, we suppose, has to be explained to those who will inherit from us in order that they might free themselves from its determinations, yet in the very project of explication we cast them – whether they be native dwellers or children – as beings of inferior intelligence to our own, beings who must perforce rely on what has been transmitted to them since they are as yet incapable of working things out for themselves.[45] Far from overcoming the presumed inequality of intelligence, the logic of reason and inheritance reproduces it.

Back to school

Human culture, in the pedagogic imagination, is an immense pyramid. At its tip is the voice of reason, singular and resplendent. With its claim to universality, reason is indifferent to variations in the experience of those who speak in its name. Transcending experience, it speaks with one voice and one alone, and all who speak with it are therefore interchangeable.[46] At the base of the pyramid, swarms of assorted memes jostle for hosts into whose mouths they will put their proverbial utterances, and into whose hands they will place their prescribed designs. These hosts, too, lack any voice they can call their own. They are but vectors, fated to broadcast the memes with which they have been infected – and anyone infected with the same meme will say the same thing. They speak not for themselves but for culture. The world according to pedagogy, in short, is a theatre of marionettes: above, reason, the master puppeteer, pulls the strings; below, a motley cast of characters, assembled from the elements of transmitted tradition, are compelled to dance to its tune. 'Reason', as philosopher Michel Serres wryly observes, 'never discovers, beneath its feet, anything but its own rule'.[47]

Consider for example the theorem of Pythagoras, that the square on the hypotenuse is equal to the sum of the squares on the opposite two sides. That it is associated with the name of Pythagoras is by the way, for in pedagogy the name no longer refers to the real historical character, shrouded in the mists of time, but has instead come to stand for the quintessence of abstract mathematical reason, to which the theorem is an eternal monument. And for this purpose, in principle, any name would do. But what are we to make of the 'hypotenuse'? How often do any of us use the term in everyday life? Indeed for most of us, Pythagoras's theorem is just one of those things we have learned to recite at school. It is a formula for transmission, not a demonstration of reason, and in receiving it as such, and replicating it on demand, we are merely confirmed in the impression we have of ourselves as beings of inferior intelligence, at least in comparison to mathematicians. That it includes such an esoteric word as hypotenuse – a word seldom heard today outside of the closed circle of the theorem and its recitation – merely serves to confirm its remoteness from experience. The theorem seems to exist, in Dewey's words, 'in a world by itself, unassimilated to ordinary customs of thought and expression'.[48]

Dewey, you will recall, thought we should commence our comprehension of what education is all about not from school but from life. The problem with school education, in his estimation, was that it has a way of isolating what is taught from the crucible of lived experience in which real knowledge is generated. The result is a tendency to reduce knowledge to information, conveyed by means of verbal and other symbolic forms the meanings of which are lost upon those who have no opportunity to participate in the practices that may, in past times and remote places, have originally given rise to them. Hypotenuse might have been part of the everyday vernacular for ancient Greek builders, but it is no longer so for today's schoolchildren. There is a standing danger, Dewey warned, that as schools become increasingly dedicated to the transmission of information in this isolated form, what is taught and learned in them will be split apart from everyday life, leading to a bifurcation between technical excellence and ordinary knowledge by which the landscape of education will cease to be one of continuous variation, giving way instead to spikes of expertise, sticking up from a homogeneous and isotropic base of common sense.[49] Surveying the scene a century after Dewey was writing, it is evident that his prophecy has been catastrophically fulfilled.

It would be wrong however to go to the other extreme, and wish for a society without schools. Perhaps we are trapped in a vicious circle: perhaps we need schools only because we have them, and because we have built a society founded upon the qualifications that they alone can provide. But it is a circle from which we are no more able to break out than we can take ourselves back to an imagined past when everything anyone needed to know could be learned through participation in the life of the community. Whether this was ever so is moot; but it is certainly no longer so today. The world we presently inhabit is so complex, and places such diverse demands on its inhabitants, that some such institution is indispensable. Moreover if formal schooling is available and necessary for some, it must be so for all, lest those who do not benefit are left at a permanent disadvantage, unable to enjoy the life-chances of their school-educated contemporaries. The question, as Dewey made very clear, is not one of how to eliminate the school but of how to strike the right balance between formal and informal modes of education.[50] And there was no doubt in his mind, and in ours today, that the balance has tipped disastrously onto the side of formal schooling.

One consequence of this imbalance is the tendency to think of education exclusively in the language of pedagogy, and to seek its preconditions in capacities of symbolisation often considered unique to humans. This is what predisposes anthropologists, working in societies without schools, to look for education in the transmission of symbolically encoded information, for example in contexts of storytelling. Initially in the possession of seniors, it is supposed that information is progressively released to juniors whose mental capacities are innately primed to receive it. Thus the original difference between juniors and seniors is gradually erased as the former are 'topped up' to the level of the latter, only for the process to be repeated in the next generation. But if that were so – if the only possible inter-generational difference were between degrees of inheritance, or between knowing more or less of a pre-existing repertoire – then social life itself would be stultified. Cut off from the very source of its nourishment, it would be stuck in a groove of ever-repeating cycles from which only accidental errors of transmission could offer hope of escape. Yet despite their stultifying effect, the metaphors of transmission and inheritance have continued to monopolise our thinking, not just in anthropology but across the entire spectrum of the human sciences. Far from respecting difference, these metaphors cast it as varying degrees of ignorance, or of mistaken or irrational belief, vis-à-vis the omniscience of scientific reason that would put a stop to the process of commoning and eradicate all difference, if only it had the power to do so.

In this chapter I have argued, with Dewey, against the counterposition of reason and inheritance that underwrites the dominant model of pedagogy. This model, in effect, drives a wedge between ways of knowing and the knowledges they convey. Who knows is one thing; the content of what is known is another. Pedagogy, then, enacts its own method, which can in principle be specified independently of both the who and the what of education. It is tantamount to a method of transmission, judged in terms of its efficiency not in growing persons or their knowledges but in transcribing pre-existent content from head to head. It is my contention, to the contrary, that the first place to find education is not in pedagogy but in participatory practice: not in the ways persons and things are symbolically represented in their absence, but in the ways they are made present, and above all answerable to one another, in the correspondences of social life. Knowledge grows along lines of correspondence: in commoning, wherein they join; and in variation, wherein each comes into its own. Every way of knowing, then, is a distinct life-line, a biographical trajectory. It follows that becoming knowledgeable is part and parcel of becoming the person you are. This is what brings it about that when you think, it is with *your* mind and no one else's; that when you speak it is with *your* voice; that when you write it is with *your* hand. Democratic education, in short, is the production not of anonymity but of difference. It is not what makes us human, for as creatures born of man and woman we are all human to begin with. It is what allows us humans collectively to make ourselves, each in his or her way. It is a process not of becoming human but of *human becoming*. And as I shall show in the next chapter, this means that we should cease regarding education as a method of transmission, and think of it rather as a practice of attention.

Notes

1 David and Ann James Premack (1994) make a strong case for confining pedagogy in the strict sense to human beings. But the matter remains contentious, with some authors claiming to have observed teaching among chimpanzees (Boesch 1991), and others finding it even more widely distributed in the animal kingdom (Caro and Hauser 1992). Much hinges on finer points of definition, as between emulation, imitation and teaching proper (Boesch and Tomasello 1998, Boesch 2003). For a recent review, see Gärdenfors and Högberg (2017).

2 On learning to make stone tools, see Stout (2005); on learning to navigate by star charts, see Lewis (1975) and Turnbull (1991).

3 See, for example, the essays in Bloch (2005). For a critique, see Ingold (2001).

4 Dewey (1966). The book was first published in 1916.

5 Dewey (1966: 1).

6 Dewey (1966: 2).

7 Dewey (1966: 4), emphases in the original.

8 Dewey (1966: 4). The key point, as educational theorist Gert Biesta observes in commenting on Dewey's text, is that common understanding is *not* a condition for participation: 'It is not that we first need to come to a common understanding and only then

begin to coordinate our actions. For Dewey it is precisely the other way around: common understanding is produced by, is the outcome of successful cooperation in action' (Biesta 2013: 30).

9 The Canadian writer and activist Heather Menzies speaks of commoning in just this sense, as 'a way of doing and organizing things as implicated participants ... *immersed in the here and now of living habitat*' (Menzies 2014: 122–123, original emphasis). See also Bollier and Helfrich (2015), who entitle their collection *Patterns of Commoning.*

10 'The experience', as Dewey put it, 'has to be formulated in order to be communicated. To formulate requires ... considering what points of contact it has with the life of another so that it may be got into such a form that he can appreciate its meaning. ... One has to assimilate, imaginatively, something of another's experience in order tell him intelligently of one's own experience. All communication is like art' (Dewey 1966: 5–6).

11 Dewey (1966: 13).

12 Dewey (1966: 11). Of course, Dewey could just as well have written of 'the things with which a *woman* varies...'. Throughout this book, wherever the gender of the person is immaterial, as it principally is, I have used masculine and feminine pronouns interchangeably – sometimes one, sometimes the other.

13 I have drawn the phrase 'response ability' from the writings of the composer John Cage (2011: 10). See also Biesta (2006: 70).

14 Dewey (1966: 42–43, 51).

15 In an eponymous volume, Alphonso Lingis speaks of 'the community of those who have nothing in common' (Lingis 1994). Community is about being, not having. In similar vein, Jean-Luc Nancy insists that we acknowledge the proper meaning of 'being-in-common' as '*in-* common or *with*', and not 'a Being or an essence of the common' (Nancy 2000: 55, original emphases). On the etymology of community as 'giving together', see Esposito (2012). 'Members of a community are bound', Esposito writes, 'by the duty of a reciprocal gift ... that conducts them outside of themselves in order to address the other' (2012: 49).

16 Dewey (1966: 22).

17 For a detailed account of the genealogical model, see Ingold (2000: 134–139).

18 This confusion between the genealogical model and the recitation of genealogies is exemplified in Philippe Descola's discussion of transmission in his magnum opus, *Beyond Nature and Culture* (2013: 329–333). For Descola, transmission is 'above all what allows the dead, through filiation, to gain a hold over the living' (2013: 329). It is the weight of ancestral past that ever presses on their descendants in the present, 'passed on inexorably from one generation to the next' (2013: 331). This is to employ the word 'transmission' in the original Deweyan sense of the continuity of life. The sense of transmission underpinning the genealogical model, however, is just the opposite. It precludes any acknowledgement of what the present owes to the past for its continuation, nor are the people of the present tasked with carrying on the work of their forbears. For with transmission in this sense, what is 'passed on' is not the current of life itself but the specifications for living it. For a more extended critique, see Ingold (2016a: 317–318).

19 For a diagrammatic depiction, see Figure 4.6 in Ingold (2007: 118).

20 Rivers's article, 'The genealogical method of anthropological inquiry', was first published in 1910 (Rivers 1968). See Ingold (2007: 109–116).

21 See, for example, Bamford and Leach (2009).

22 This idea of gene–culture coevolution has given rise to an extensive literature. Representative examples are Durham (1991), Richerson and Boyd (2008), and Paul (2015).

23 Oyama (1985: 13).

24 In this paragraph I have summarised arguments set out at greater length in Ingold (2002).

25 Dewey (1966: 34).

26 To the best of my knowledge, this idea was first proposed in 1978 by Peter Richerson and Robert Boyd, in a founding contribution to the theory of gene–culture evolution. 'To predict the phenotype of a cultural organism one must know its genotype, its

environment and its "culture-type", the cultural message that the organism received from other individuals of the same species' (Richerson and Boyd 1978: 128).

27 Dewey (1966: 34).

28 All direct quotations in this paragraph are from Dewey (1966: 11).

29 See Dawkins (1976) and Blackmore (2000). For examples of earlier proposals for a cultural analogue of the gene, and references to these, see Ingold (2016b: 299).

30 Sperber (1996).

31 Sperber (1996: 61).

32 Dewey (1966: 14).

33 Ingold (2001: 137).

34 Dewey (1966: 4–5).

35 Ingold (2000: 198–201).

36 Ingold (2001: 137–138).

37 An example is Donna Eder's (2007) sensitive account of indigenous Navajo storytelling, and its transferability to the institutional context of the western school. While stressing the importance of focusing on the practices of telling as well as the content of what is told, Eder nevertheless holds that the purpose of the stories is to convey a set of implicit beliefs and meanings that together enshrine the 'principles necessary to live well' (Eder 2007: 279, 288). The beliefs and meanings are already there, buried in the story texts, even before their narration.

38 Ingold (2011: 162).

39 The phrase 'growing older together' comes from the social phenomenology of Alfred Schütz, who used it to describe how consociates, such as parents and children, 'are mutually involved in one another's biography' (Schütz 1962: 16–17).

40 Dewey (1966: 38).

41 In *The Invention of Culture*, first published in 1975, Roy Wagner offers a classic account of how each sense of culture precipitates the other (Wagner 2016: 21–27).

42 See Tylor (1871, I: 1); Lowie (1937: 3).

43 Lowie (1921: 428).

44 The critical literature surrounding science and traditional knowledge is extensive. Exemplary discussions can be found in Agrawal (1995), Cruikshank (1998: 45–70), Ingold and Kurttila (2000) and Nadasdy (2003).

45 This is the argument of philosopher Jacques Rancière (1991), to which we will return.

46 The community of reason, as Biesta puts it, 'is constituted by a common language and a common logic. It gives us a voice, but only a representative voice. ... Although it does matter *what* we say, it does not matter *who* is saying it, because in the rational community we are interchangeable' (Biesta 2006: 62, emphases in the original).

47 Serres (1997: xiii).

48 Dewey (1966: 8).

49 Dewey (1966: 8–9).

50 'One of the weightiest problems with which the philosophy of education has to cope is the method of keeping a proper balance between the informal and the formal, the incidental and the intentional, modes of education' (Dewey 1996: 9).

2

FOR ATTENTION

The principle of habit

We human beings don't just live our lives. We lead them. That's the difference between *bios* and *zōē*, between life lived as a story, and life bound to the cycles of nature.[1] Whether non-human animals, at least of some kinds, might also lead their lives is a question for which we currently have no certain answer, and while of great interest and importance, I shall not address it here. What presently concerns me is the difference, the excess of leading over living, not the issue of where to draw the line, if indeed any can be drawn, between life-leading and life-living creatures. I want to know what it means to lead life, in what sense it surpasses what already exists, in what sense it has a past and a future, and a notion of its own direction. For that, I contend, is fundamentally the question of education. The word 'education', after all, is derived from the Latin *ducere*, 'to lead', though the significance of the 'e' that prefixes it is a more tricky matter to which I shall return. In the last chapter I argued that leading life is not about transmission. On the contrary, transmission shuts life down, confining it to the replication of already existing routines. At best it is a modality of training, not of education. In this chapter I argue that what really makes the difference between leading life and living it is *attention*.

As with 'education', it pays to note the derivation of the word, which once again we owe to Latin. 'Attention' comes from *ad-tendere*, literally meaning to stretch (*tendere*) toward (*ad*). It is the stretch of life that I am after. We all know what this means, intuitively, when we strain to hear a distant sound. Though in a purely mechanical sense, the sound reaches our ears, which are firmly cemented in our heads, we have a feeling that it is we who reach out towards the source of sound, as if the entire body were itself an elastic ear that feels in its tension the effort of the stretch. We say we don't just hear but actively *listen*.[2] That is one meaning of attending. But the word has a host of related meanings that are equally important for what I shall have to say. These include: *caring* for people or for things, in a way that is both practical and dutiful; *waiting*, in the expectation of a call or summons; *being present*, or coming into presence, as on an occasion; and *going along* with others, as in joining or accompanying. Besides all these, however, I would like to give an additional meaning to the stretch of life – a temporal one – by which, with *bios*, life is not merely lived in the here and now but is stretched by a memory of the future that itself allows every present moment to be a new beginning. For this imaginative remembering, or mnemonic imagining, I shall introduce the term 'longing'. Longing, in my usage, is another word for the stretching of a life, along a line.

To begin, however, I would like to return to John Dewey, and to what he had to say about the continuity of life, specifically in his later work on *Art as Experience*.[3] Here he deliberates at length on the significance of two terms which will also be of great importance to my argument, namely 'doing' and 'undergoing'.[4] In every experience, Dewey tells us, there has to be an element of both. The problem is to figure out the relation between them, for in the perception of this relation lies the work of consciousness. It cannot be that they merely alternate, for if that were so, there could be no pattern to experience: it would be no more than a series of disconnected episodes. Dewey's point is that life is continuous, rather than episodic, precisely because undergoing is not confined within, but rather overflows, every doing. Thus the actions we undertake in the world – the things we do – take into themselves and draw some of their meaning from what we have undergone in the course of previous doings, or suffered under the environing conditions these doings have induced. And conversely, what we presently undergo in carrying out these actions, and the environmental consequences they bring in train, bear upon further doing. The process of living, to quote Dewey at length,

> possesses continuity because it is an everlastingly renewed process of acting upon the environment and being acted upon by it, together with institution of relations between what is done and what is undergone. ... The world we have experienced becomes an integral part of the self that acts and is acted upon in further experience. In their physical occurrence, things and events experienced pass and are gone. But something of their meaning and value is retained as an integral part of the self. Through habits formed in intercourse with the world, we also in-habit the world. It becomes a home and the home is part of our every experience.[5]

In this passage, besides 'doing' and 'undergoing', Dewey introduces a third term which will also be critical to the argument I develop here. This is 'habit'. The term is notoriously ambiguous, commonly referring at once to what makes people do things, and to what is formed in them in consequence of their repeatedly doing them.[6] Do we make habit, or does habit make us? Are we, so to speak, in front of habit or behind it? Dewey's answer to the conundrum is to suppose that we are neither in front nor behind, but in the midst. In effect, he resolves the ambiguity by shifting the register from cause and consequence to process. Thus habit, for Dewey, is neither producer nor product but the *principle of production*, whereby a self that dwells in its own practices is recursively generated by them. As such, habit is what undergoing brings to the task of doing. In one of his last published statements on the theme of education – his lectures on *Experience and Education* dating from 1938 – Dewey returns to the question of habit. Taking care to distinguish habit as *principle* from what we might ordinarily think of as *a* habit, meaning an already fixed and settled way of doing things, Dewey explains that according to this principle,

> every experience enacted and undergone modifies the one who acts and undergoes, while this modification affects, whether we wish it or not, the quality of subsequent experiences. For it is a somewhat different person who enters into them.[7]

Once again, Dewey characterises experience through the conjunction of doing and undergoing. And again, what for him defines habit is a specific relation between the two, whereby all doing is carried in the undergoing. To appreciate the import of this principle, we have only to imagine what the consequence would be, were the relation to be inverted. What would happen if every undergoing were subtended by an act of doing, rather than vice versa? The inversion would, in effect, yield a principle that is the very opposite of that of habit: we could call it the *principle of volition*. According to this principle, every act would deliver on an intention wilfully placed before it. The doing would begin here, with an intention in the mind of an agent, and end there, with that intention fulfilled in the world. Between beginning and ending there are, of course, things the doer has to undergo – and possibly not only the doer, but also others subject to his command and enrolled in his project. All are bound to endure its effects, and may indeed be changed by them. But so long as the undergoing is inside the doing it is passively borne, for the active part of conduct is defined by its ends, its finalities. With the principle of volition, in short, doing and undergoing are set apart on opposite sides of a division between the active and the passive, agency and patiency.

With the principle of habit, however, this opposition is dissolved. Here, undergoing is what one does, and doing what one undergoes. Active undergoing continually digests the ends of doing, and extrudes them into pure beginning. In Dewey's terms, the digestion is a 'taking in', the extrusion a 'going out'. Thus what he called 'the undergoing phase of experience', though on the one hand it 'involves surrender', on the other hand entails 'the going-out of energy in order to receive, not a withholding of energy'. Were we but passive in the midst of experience we would be overwhelmed by it and incapable of answering to it. 'We must summon energy and pitch it at a responsive key', Dewey continues, 'in order to take in'.[8] I call this summoning and pitching 'correspondence', another term at the heart of my argument in this chapter. With correspondence, we are not so much changed from without as transformed from within. The doing is *inside* the undergoing. That's what distinguishes it as an enactment of *experience*, for to enact an experience – in anything other than a banal dramaturgical sense – is to be always already inside it, that is to *inhabit* it. Thus through doing undergoing, as Dewey recognised, we inhabit the world. And the thesis I wish to defend, in the following paragraphs, is that in its lively responsiveness, this habitation is fundamentally a process of attention.

Taking a walk

Suppose for example that I go for a walk. It is something I intend to do, and I get ready by planning a route, putting on my boots and packing a map and provisions in a knapsack. My plan is to take a tour of the countryside, and perhaps to improve my physical fitness and sense of wellbeing from the exercise. I also want to do some thinking. These ends are already there at the beginning, albeit as yet unfulfilled. I am aware that in their fulfilment I might have to suffer a bit: quite apart from aching legs and possible blisters, there is the sheer monotony of putting one foot before the other, over and over again. But as I reassure myself, walking is just a habit; it is sedimented in my body and I can do it more or less without thinking. Thought comes into it only with hazardous passages or at moments when I might have to stop to check my directions or choose which path to take. In between whiles, I can get on with thinking in my head and leave the rest of my body to look after itself: as everyone knows, walking is good for meditation, perhaps because of its steady rhythm, perhaps because of the temporary respite it affords from the demands that otherwise press on us from all sides. Regarded from this angle, what the walk offers is a space between the fixed points of origin and destination, a space for both mental and physical exertion that I hope will yield results. The idea of going for a walk, in order to achieve these results, fully accords with the principle of volition.

But once embarked on my walk, this account no longer works as it did before setting out. Walking ceases to be something that I set my body to do, as a self-imposed routine. Rather, it seems that I *become* my walking, and that my walking walks me.[9] I am there, inside of it, animated by its movement. And with every step I am not so much changed as modified, in the sense not of transition from one state to another but of perpetual renewal. I am indeed a different person when I arrive; not the same person in another place, or with a body marked by the stigmata of passage. Even the aches and the blisters unfold in my experience, as part of a life actively undergone, and may be all the more painful for that: like it or not, I cannot detach them from the walking being that I am. They are biographical, and I can tell a story from them.[10] Nor, once on my way, can I sustain the idea that walking is thought-less, a bodily automatism that frees the mind to do its own thing. On the contrary, walking is itself a habit of thinking. This thinking is not however an inside-the-head, cognitive operation but the work of a mind that, in its deliberations, freely mingles with the body and the world. Or to put it another way, I do not so much think *while* walking as think *in* walking.[11] This thinking is a way of taking in the world, so that it becomes less the topic than the medium of my meditation. Perhaps the meditative power of walking lies in precisely this: that it gives thought room to breathe, to let the world in on its reflections. But by the same token, to be open to the world we must also surrender something of our agency. We must become responsive beings. Thus, even as I walk, I must adjust my footing to the terrain, follow the path, submit to the elements. There is, in every step, an element of uncertainty.

This, I suppose, is what it means to *inhabit* the practice of walking. It is to put the 'I' who acts in the midst of the experience undergone, rather than in advance of it. The volitional 'I' is an unwelcome intruder in the doing of undergoing: intent on imposing its own directions, it keeps butting in, dictating ends before beginnings, insisting on a regime of stop and start in which every act follows in sequence from the completion of its predecessor. The 'I' of habit, by contrast, falls in the slipstream of action. Here, ends are not given in advance but emerge in the action itself, and are recognisable as such only in acknowledging the possibility of new beginnings. Beginnings *produce* endings, and are produced by them. Amidst this production, at once of self and world, the 'I' is continually in question. It is no longer possible to say, with confidence, 'I do this' or 'I did that'. One has rather to ask, 'is this what I am doing?', or 'did I do that?' It is as if the action were ever calling for my agency in its wake, not as an answer but as a question. 'I am', as philosopher Erin Manning puts it, is always, to a large degree, 'was that me?'[12] The principle of habit asserts that one is never fully the master of one's own acts; that to lead life is not necessarily to be in command. Indeed to presume mastery in any situation of existential uncertainty is to court disaster. Failure to respond to the exigencies of a situation can wreck the best-laid plans. But just because not everything happens according to one's own volition does not mean that someone else is in charge, or that agency is more widely distributed. It means, rather, that there must be something wrong with an account of action that presumes that whatever happens to us is an effect of some agency or other.[13] What if, instead, we were to install the principle of habit?

If agency is not given in advance of action, as cause to effect, but is rather ever forming and transforming from within the action itself, then perhaps we should turn the noun into the gerund of a verb, and agree to speak of 'becoming agent', or 'agencing'. The equivalent in French, often considered untranslatable, is *agencement*. I shall not venture further on the semantic potential of this term here, as it will come up again in the next chapter. Suffice it to say that it is more or less equivalent to what I introduced earlier as 'doing undergoing'. The principle of habit, then, substitutes *agencement* for agency. The difference is that whereas agency belongs to us, as beings endowed with volition, *agencement* falls to us, as dwellers in habit. The first is a property we allegedly possess that enables us to act; the second is a task we are bound to take on as responsive and responsible beings, and as part of the life we undergo. Put in the most general terms, life itself is a task, and to lead it, as *bios* rather than *zōē*, is the task of education.[14] That is why Dewey insisted on placing education within the realm of habit. 'The result of the educative process', as he put it, can only be a 'capacity for further education'.[15]

Attentionality and correspondence

We now have two alternative triads, the terms of each of which are tightly bound by mutual implication. On the one hand is the triad: volition, agency, intentionality.[16] On the other is the triad: habit, *agencement*, attentionality. I have explained the difference between the principles of volition and habit, and between agency and *agencement*. The next step is to consider the distinction between intention and attention. To begin, let me return to my example of taking a walk. My first account, of *going for a walk*, was couched in terms of my intentions: to see the countryside, improve my fitness and wellbeing and do some thinking. Of course there are things I have to attend to, both in preparation and during the walk itself. But this attention is the way the mind has of checking up on the world. It interrupts movement in order to take stock. Before setting out I check that I have everything I need: map, compass, rations, and so on. It is like ticking things off from a list I already have in my head. En route, I check that features of the visible landscape match what is marked on the map, allowing me to confirm my topographical position. And where there are potential hazards, I check that I have the right manoeuvre to circumvent them. In short, attention is about matching up the contents of the mind with objects in the world, and establishing a one-to-one correlation between each mental representation and each physical feature.[17] This is the form of attention when our fundamental way of being in the world is understood to be intentional. And it is accordingly framed by the principle of volition.

But in my second account, of *walking*, which is framed by the principle of habit, the relation between intention and attention is the other way about. Walking, as we have seen, calls for the pedestrian's continual responsiveness to the terrain, the path and the elements. To respond, he must attend to these things *as he goes along*, joining or participating with them in his own movements. This is what it means to listen, watch and feel. If attention, in our first account, interrupts or cuts across movement so as to establish a transverse relation between mind and world (the separation of which is assumed from the outset), in the second it joins *with* the movement as an accompaniment or refrain. Attention, in this sense, is longitudinal. The attentive walker tunes his movement to the terrain as it unfolds around him and beneath his feet, rather than having to stop at intervals to check up on it. And if the opposite of attention is distraction, then the same distinction holds. In one account, distraction entails a loss of mental focus, a blurring of the objects of attention caused, more often than not, by the intrusions of the body into conscious awareness, whether due to the afflictions of sore feet and aching legs, or to the jarring and jolting to which it is subjected by uneven ground or other extraneous impacts. The mind attends; the body distracts.[18] But in the other account, distraction is a diversion of the entire being in its environment. While following one path, the walker may be drawn to another which leads him off track, perhaps even causing him to lose his way. Distraction, here, is a deviation of the line of attention, not the occlusion of its target. This is the distraction of the lure, which attracts, captivates and ultimately immobilises its victim in a mesh of lines that, going every which way, leave him literally spellbound.

Now my contention is that in the habit of walking, as opposed to the volition of going for a walk, attentionality takes ontological priority as the fundamental mode of being in the world, whereas intentions are but milestones thrown up along the way, more often than not revealed in hindsight when, looking back on a trip already made, we reconstruct it as a series of predetermined stages. Or to put it in a nutshell, if the principle of volition renders a form of attention founded in intentionality, the principle of habit gives us a form of intention founded in attentionality. I do not mean to deny that a mind is at work in the attentionality of walking, just as it is in the intentionality of going for a walk. But this is not a mind confined to the head and set over against the world; it is rather one that extends along the sensory pathways of the pedestrian's participation in the environment.[19] The awareness of such a mind is not transitive but intransitive, not *of* but *with*. Where 'of-ness' makes the other to which one attends into its object, and ticks it off, '*with*-ness' saves the other from objectification by bringing it alongside as a companion or accomplice. It turns othering into togethering. To start with the principle of habit, rather than that of volition, is to acknowledge that awareness is always awareness *with* before it is ever awareness *of*. We can recognise a movement, and respond to it, before we ever fix it in our sights. The operations of the attentional mind, in short, are not cognitive but ecological. In the light of this conclusion, I now want to return to a term that turned out to be key to my discussion in the last chapter – namely *correspondence* – and to link it to what I have just said about attentionality.

First, let me dispose of the meaning of correspondence that I do *not* intend with the term. I do not mean the matching of one set of elements, such as concepts in the mind, with another set, such as objects in the world, by some principle of homology that leads any one element in the first set to equate with one or more elements in the second, and vice versa. This is what correspondence means in mathematics, and there is of course a close affinity between this meaning and the sense of attention as a transverse correlation between concept and object.[20] What I *do* intend with correspondence can be readily grasped by comparing this transverse sense of attention with its sense as a longitudinal 'going along with'. It is the process by which beings or things quite literally co-respond or answer to one another over time, as for example in the exchange of letters or of words in conversation. It is comprised, as we saw in Chapter 1, of the co-dependency of commoning and variation, of the way in which every being finds its singular voice in the sharing of experience with others. The claim I want to make is that correspondence is the way of relating of a being that dwells in habit and whose stance is attentional. For it is in attending to one another, as they go along together, that beings correspond.

It is necessary here to insert a clear analytic distinction between correspondence and interaction.[21] You could compare it to the difference between two companions walking along together, facing the same way, and an interview situation, or perhaps a board game, in which participants face each other across the table. In a game of chess, for example, the players alternate in their moves – back-and-forth and hand-over-hand – and each move is ostensibly a discrete, deliberate and considered act, the result of which is to change the configuration of the board. In taking turns in acts that target the other, the players appear to be engaged in a rudimentary form of interaction. For not only are their separate identities and interests given from the start, they also make no attempt to find common cause. Each keeps to himself; there is neither commoning nor variation. Every move, in chess, is not so much a submission as a declaration of intent: its purpose to frustrate, and ultimately to check, the progress of one's opponent. Thus as the game proceeds, each 'I' gets in the way of the other until it ends in the 'mate' of total gridlock. Behind the appearance of interaction, however, lies a different reality. For in truth, both players together *inhabit* the game of chess: they are drawn to it, captivated by it, and open up to one another in their shared love of the game and the fellow feeling that allows them to play in a spirit of friendship.[22] Their common experience develops hand in hand with their personal styles of playing. They might well have a sense, as they move their respective pieces, that their hand answers to something beyond them and wonder afterwards, 'did I do that?' or 'was that me?' Their agency, in short, is always in question, not determined in advance. What is at stake, in practice, is not the opposition of their agency but the alignment of their *agencement*. And in this sense, the players are, after all, as much correspondents in the game as are walking companions on the trail.

Care and longing

I now turn to two other aspects of attentionality which, like correspondence, are crucial to our conception of what it means to lead life, and therefore of education. These are *care* and *longing*. The first brings an ethical dimension to attention. Naturally, we care for people and things by giving them our full attention and by responding to their needs. As co-responsive beings, the responsibility of care is something that *falls* to us. The actions we carry out in its fulfilment are therefore in the nature of tasks. A task is an action that we *owe* rather than *own*: it belongs to others rather than ourselves. As much undergone as done, it is a 'doing undergoing' which comes to us because we are people of habit. It is not done of our own free will, but nor is it obligatory in the sense that it is imposed upon us by some higher order of society to which we are similarly accountable. Rather, it is done because in a 'community of those who have nothing in common' – that is in a community bound by emergent difference rather than prior identity, in which everyone is to some degree a stranger to everyone else – their presence *demands* a response. As the theorist of education Gert Biesta has written, 'what is done, what needs to be done, and what only I can do, is to *respond* to the stranger, to be *responsive* and *responsible* to what the stranger asks from me'.[23] There can, in this sense, be no responsibility without 'response ability'. To be answerable, one must be able to answer. And to be able to answer, one must be present. In the language of commoning and variation, in which each person speaks with his or her unique and singular voice rather than as a representative of the collectivity, what matters is not so much the words we use as that we should respond with them. For it is by way of our words, and the voices with which we utter them, that we make ourselves present to others as the particular persons we are. [24]

To care for others, then, we must allow them into our presence so that we, in turn, can be present to them. In an important sense, we must let them be, so that they can speak to us. However letting be, in this sense, is not easily reconciled with understanding, let alone with explanation. Understanding and explanation belong to that other mode of attention, as check-up. In this mode, we attend to things and persons so that we can *account* for them. Once accounted for, they can be ticked off, removed from our list and dispatched to that repository of the 'already known' or 'well understood', the contents of which no longer demand anything of us. And this, so often, is how we encounter them, not least in the institutionalised settings and practices of education. How often have we heard it said, by learned and compassionate humanists, that understanding depends on embedding things in their contexts, whether social, cultural or historical? It is like putting them to sleep. To the rebellious child, who refuses to lie down and go to sleep and keeps leaping out of bed, do we issue the command: 'get back into your proper context and be understood?' Truly, what the child wants, and indeed demands, is attention. He or she has things to say, to tell us or to show us, and cries out to be noticed. And we should watch, listen and respond. That is what it means to care.

The implication of this argument, however, is radical. It means that if education is about caring for the world we live in, and for its multiple human and non-human inhabitants, then it is not so much about understanding them as it is about restoring them to presence, so that we can attend and respond to what they have to say. Indeed philosophers Jan Masschelein and Maarten Simons, in their defence of the educational purpose of the school (of which more below, Chapter 3), make precisely this point. There is a 'magical moment', they say, when things which used only to be talked about or discussed, as it were in their absence, suddenly become present and active in their own right and start to talk themselves. Spellbound, we listen. It is the purpose of the school, argue Masschelein and Simons, to make things real again in this sense, and to restore them to our attention.[25] There is however a still wider point to be made in this connection. It is that care entails not just listening to what others have to tell us, but also responding in kind. It is a matter of discharging an ontological debt, of giving back to the world and its inhabitants what we owe them for our own formation. That which we owe is, in the original sense of the term, a *duty*. That is why the responsibility of care is not only practical (there are tasks to be undertaken) but dutiful (it discharges a debt). It follows that education – leading life – is not done out of volition, nor under obligation, but as the discharge of duty.

What have care and attention, then, to do with longing? The answer lies in the way longing brings together the activities of remembering and imagining. Both are ways of presencing: remembering presences the past; imagining the future. By remembering, here, I do not mean making the past into an *object* of memory. That would be tantamount to separating the past from the present, as if it were complete, over and done with, and available for transmission as heritable property. This is what happens when we put the past in its context. The entire context, then, along with everything embedded in it, becomes part of the package. In remembering, to the contrary, the past is not finished but active in the present. To remember, in practice, is to re-enter as a correspondent in the processes of one's own and others' development. It is to pick up the threads of past lives and to join *with* them in finding a way forward. Even if people who have passed away can be remembered only by their stories, every telling is not just *about* the person told: in a real sense it *is* the person, with their unique voice and character, brought into the here and now so that the living can carry on a correspondence with them. Storytelling in this sense is a prolongation of the *bios*, not a way of wrapping it up. And that is just another way of saying that it is a form of longing.

So it is too with imagining. For if remembering does not make the past an object, then nor does imagining make an object of the future. That is to say, it is not to *project* the future, as a state of affairs distinct from the present. It is rather to catch a life that, in its hopes and dreams, has a way of running ahead of its moorings in the material world. Where it runs is beyond the horizon of our conceptualisation. Thinkers of all professions, wrote Dewey in *Art as Experience*, whether they be poets or painters, scientists or philosophers, in their imaginings 'press forward toward some end dimly and imprecisely prefigured, groping their way as they are lured on by the identity of an aura in which their observations and reflections swim'.[26] In this aura, all imagining is remembering and all remembering imagining. Future and past, no longer distinguishable, merge at the ends of longing, in a place we perpetually dream of and strive for, but never reach. In short, longing makes it possible to align care and attention, which depend on bringing things into presence, with the temporal stretch of life. This is not a life that runs from here to there, from a point of origin to a destination, nor can it be marked off with milestones. Like the stretch of attentionality with which it corresponds, life runs forever in between the points that intentions join up, as a river runs between its banks. Thus no more than life can education have predetermined 'outcomes'. As Dewey has taught us, and as we observed in Chapter 1, the only outcome of life is further life, the only outcome of growth further growth, the only outcome of education further education.[27]

Attention as education and the education of attention

This, then, is the point at which to return to the theme of education, and to show how what we have said so far about attention bears on it. I shall do this by addressing the work of two scholars who have profoundly influenced the way I think about education: Jan Masschelein and James Gibson. Masschelein is a contemporary philosopher whose particular field is the philosophy of education. Gibson was a psychologist of visual perception and a pioneer of what came to be known as the ecological approach to perception and action. His most important work was published in the 1960s and 1970s. I begin, however, with some words about the word 'education' itself. I have already noted the derivation of the word from the Latin *ducere*, 'to lead'; however I left open the significance of the 'e' at the front. There is a conventional etymology, of course, that takes us back to a related Latin word, *educare*, meaning simply to teach, to rear or bring up, or to instil in each new generation the approved manners of society and the knowledge on which they rest. Masschelein, however, proposes to turn this convention on its head. What if we were to start with the 'e' of education, and rewrite education as *e-ducation*? The 'e' comes from *ex*, meaning 'out'. Education, then, would not be about instilling knowledge *in* to the minds of novices but about leading them *out* into the world.[28]

In the first sense, education – at least in its modern version – aims to provide the tools for explanation and critical reasoning. It cleaves to an ideal that the student, who begins in ignorance and must first have things explained, will eventually emerge as a thinker in his or her own right, emancipated from the conventions and prejudices of the past, and able to join the high table of those with the authority to explain. It is a passage from ignorance to intellect. Yet if the world can be known only by way of its explanations, or by the different ways in which it may be represented, and if reason teaches us to distrust all established representations and to seek a critical point of view of our own, freed from the contexts in which these representational forerunners are retrospectively understood to have been embedded, then how can we ever open to the world itself? How, as Masschelein asks, 'can we turn the world into something "real", how to make the world "present", to give again the real and discard the shields or mirrors that seem to have locked us up increasingly into self-reflections and interpretations, into endless returns upon "standpoints", "perspectives" and "opinions"?'[29] His answer is: by adopting practices which allow us, quite literally, 'to expose ourselves'.[30] And this, Masschelein contends, is the aim of e-ducation in the second sense. Its purpose is not to instil a consciousness or awareness *of* the world around us. It is rather to draw us into a correspondence *with* this world. Or in a word, it is about *attending* to it.

For a paradigmatic example of what exposure means in practice, Masschelein invites us to join him in the activity of walking. Once on the trail we submit to it – we are even commanded by it – and in that sense the walk is an experience we undergo. Yet this is not, Masschelein tells us, a 'passive undergoing'. It is active, 'a kind of cutting the road through'.[31] So what is this road, and what does it cut? The road, of course, is that of attention, along which the world opens up and is made present to us, so that we ourselves may be exposed to this presence and be transformed. As Masschelein insists, 'attention makes experience possible'.[32] And what the road cuts through are all the transitive links that connect intentions with their targets, consciousness with its objects, or critical awareness with what it is *of*. The thing about walking, according to Masschelein, is not that it offers a different perspective or set of perspectives from that which may be gained by other means (such as from the air), nor that it allows us to challenge any one point of view with others. What it does offer us is a *different relation to the present*, one that calls not for explanation, understanding, or interpretation in context, but for our undivided, unmediated and unqualified attention. Walking can do this for us because, far from enjoining us to take a stand from this position or that, it continually pulls us away from *any* standpoint – from any position we might adopt. 'Walking', as Masschelein explains, 'is about putting this position at stake; it is about ex-position, about being out-of-position'.[33] And this, precisely, is what he means by exposure.

Now at first glance Masschelein and Gibson could hardly make for a less likely comparison. Their interests, respectively in the philosophy of education and the psychology of perception, are entirely different, as are their intellectual styles and sources of inspiration. Yet if Masschelein wants to make the world real and present to us again, so does Gibson. And for Gibson, too, this means repudiating the ideas that we can only know the world from the perspective of a fixed standpoint, and only know it in full by assembling, in the mind, all partial representations – obtained from diverse standpoints – into a comprehensive picture of the whole, a kind of mental map. For Gibson, the world we perceive is a world around us, an environment. And we become familiar with this environment not by looking *at* it, or by a mental check-up that tests our representations against the evidence of the senses, but by moving around *in* it, for example by walking. In movement we follow what Gibson calls a 'path of observation', and as we move the pattern of sensory stimulus undergoes continual modulation. With vision, in which Gibson is especially interested, this is the pattern of light reflected off the surfaces of things, or what is known as the 'ambient optic array', as it meets the eyes of the moving observer. Underlying the modulations of the array are certain invariant parameters, and it is Gibson's contention that these invariants are sufficient to specify relevant features of the environment, or more precisely, to specify what they afford, in terms of possibilities or hindrances offered to the observer in following his or her course of action.[34]

Among these features are the layout and texture of the ground, and to continue with our example of walking, some sorts of ground – such as solid earth or gravel – afford walking whereas others – such as scree or swamp – do not. And according to Gibson, earth, gravel, scree and swamp are perceived, in the first place, in their walkability. Of course, the sort of familiarity with an environment that enables us to perceive walkability does not come ready-made; it grows with experience. Growing familiarity, however, comes not from filling in gaps in the map but from a gradual fine-tuning or sensitisation of perceptual skills that renders perceivers ever more attentive to the nuances of the environment. One can be an explorer on home ground, since in the real world – as opposed to the world of its representations – there is always more to be discovered. Thus novices are not so much 'filled up' – as envisaged by advocates of the transmission model of education – as 'tuned up'.[35] Otherwise put, if the knowledge of the old-hand is superior to that of the novice, it is not because he has acquired the mental representations that enable him to construct a more elaborate picture of the world, but because his perceptual system is attuned to attend to critical features of the environment that the novice simply fails to notice. Adopting one of Gibson's key metaphors, we could say that the perceptual system of the skilled practitioner *resonates* with the properties of the environment. The more practised we become in walking the paths of observation, according to Gibson, the better able we are to notice and to respond fluently to environmental variations and to the parametric invariants that underwrite them. That is to say, we undergo what he called an 'education of attention'.[36]

For both Masschelein and Gibson, then, education is fundamentally about attention, not about transmission. So are they, in their different ways, saying the same thing? Indeed they are not, and the key to their difference lies in the relation between skill and submission. These are necessarily co-present in any practice of habit, or of 'doing undergoing'. Consider again the example of the walker. He must, on the one hand, be sufficiently attentive to be able to perceive the walk-ability of the terrain, and to adjust his footwork in relation to it. He has a certain practical mastery of the art of walking, which comes with experience. But on the other hand, with every step he submits to the path with no surety of where it will lead. And when we dwell in walking, as in any other habit, it is submission that leads, whereas mastery follows in its wake, and not the other way around.[37] There is attention in both, but in one the practitioner is at the behest of the world, in the other the world is at the behest of the practitioner. One lets the world in, like a deep breath; the other lets it out in an oriented movement of perception and action. 'Experiencing like breathing', as Dewey put it, 'is a rhythm of intakings and outgoings'.[38] Masschelein is unequivocally on the side of the intake. That is why he reminds us that the word *attendre*, in French, means 'to wait'. Even in English, to attend to things or persons means waiting on them, abiding with them and follow-ing what they do.[39] Gibson, by contrast, is on the side of outgoing. In the detection of affordances, of opportunities for carrying on, practitioners pick up and turn to their advantage features of a world that is already laid out. Or in short, whereas for Masschelein the practitioner waits upon the world, for Gibson the world waits for the practitioner.[40] In the first case, attention educates by exposing us to a world in formation, by letting it in. But in the second, attention is what is educated, by dint of this experience. In truth, however, there cannot be one without the other. Submission and practical mastery are two sides of the same coin. That coin is the principle of habit.

Weak, poor and risky

'Education', declared the poet William Butler Yeats, 'is not about filling a pail but about lighting a fire'.[41] The pail offers certainty and predictability, a starting point and an end point, with measurable steps along the way. It has outcomes, which should be known and understood even before the process begins. The fire, on the other hand, exposes us all to risk. There is no knowing what will ignite and what will not, for how long the fire will burn, how it will spread, and what its outcomes will be. In his recent book *The Beautiful Risk of Education*, Gert Biesta expresses the choice as one between essence and existence, or in other words, between meta-physics and life.[42] In the metaphysical register, we appeal to some essence of trans-cendent humanity. Education, then, is the process of becoming human, of instilling into the raw material of immature human beings the knowledge, norms, values and responsibilities of personhood and civil society. That is to fill the pail. But to choose existence is to restore humans to a process of life lived in company with others, that is, to *social* life. Existence – life – is not a process of *becoming human*; it is rather one of *human becoming*.[43] The question of education, as Biesta puts it, is whether we are prepared to take the risk of life, with all its uncertainty, unpredictability and frustra-tion, or whether we prefer to seek a certainty beyond or subtending life, on the level of metaphysics. The choice is between what he calls a strong and a weak way of education. The strong way offers security, predictability and freedom from risk.

The weak way, by contrast, is slow, difficult and by no means certain in its results – if indeed we can speak of 'results' at all. We live in an age when politicians, policy makers and the public are vociferous in their demands that education should be strong. Weakness is perceived as a problem. Biesta's contention, to the contrary, is that if we take the weakness out of education, we are in danger of taking out education altogether.[44] To do so would be to extinguish the fire.

It should by now be readily apparent that this distinction between strong and weak ways of education is virtually congruent with the one from which I began this chapter, between the principles of volition and habit. The volitional principle sets ends before beginning, and aims to bring about a change of state in those subjected to it and compelled to undergo its impositions. In the case of education, this is nothing less than the installation of a human essence. It is as though education were on the inside of a once-and-for all moment of creation, destined to recapitulate in every generation the genesis of humanity in the transition from nature to society. The principle of habit, on the contrary, rather than starting from ends, produces beginnings. Its creativity is that of 'doing undergoing', of *agencement*, in which beings continually forge themselves and one another in the crucible of social life, their humanity not a foregone conclusion but an ongoing relational achievement. The theologian Henry Nelson Wieman referred to it as the kind of creativity that 'progressively creates personality in community'. Behind the contingencies of what people do, Wieman argued, and the miscellany of products or 'created goods' to which these doings give rise, is a 'creative good' intrinsic to human life in its capacity to generate persons in relationships. This kind of creativity, he writes, is 'what personality undergoes but cannot do'.[45] It does not begin, as the volitional principle would have it, with an intention in mind and end with its fulfilment. Rather it carries on through, every loose end offering the possibility of new beginning for those who follow on. Such is the creativity of social life. Biesta, too, draws much the same contrast, between a strong notion of creation as a transition 'from non-being to being', and a weak notion of creation as 'calling being to life'.[46] If education, in the strong sense, recreates the essence of humanity, what it continually creates, in the weak sense, is human existence.

Though we may all be humans by birth, the strong logic of *becoming human* implies that some are nevertheless more human than others. Children in their 'early years', closer to their point of origin, having only recently started on the road to humanity, are considered less human than adults on approach to full qualification. Now it is the mission of education in the strong sense (from *educare*) to raise every child from an original state of naivety and release him or her into the freedom of adult intelligence. Yet as we saw in Chapter 1, far from eliminating inequality, this project of emancipation perpetuates it. It does so by inserting, from the start, a division between those of inferior intellect (not only children, but also people in 'traditional societies' and the 'common man' in our own), who stand in need of liberation, and those of superior intellect (grown-ups, scientists and people of Culture) whose mission it is to liberate them. The former will in turn become emancipators, but only to place their successors in a position of inferiority, so that the cycle can begin again. What the philosopher Jacques Rancière calls the 'myth of pedagogy' tells of a world divided: between 'knowing minds and ignorant ones … the capable and incapable, the intelligent and the stupid'.[47] Having decreed a ground zero, an absolute point of origin for the educational process, the pedagogue throws a veil of ignorance over everything to be learned, only to appoint himself to the task of lifting it. This task, according to Rancière, is to *explicate*: that is, 'to transmit learning and form minds simultaneously, by leading those minds, according to an ordered progression, from the most simple to the most complex'.[48] But the logic of explica-tion yields an infinite regress. Once a thing is explained, then it becomes necessary to explain the explanation, and so on, leaving the recipient of the explanation, the benighted pupil, ever further behind, and giving greater urgency to the need to 'catch up', to recover the distance that the logic of explication has itself set up. And what does the pupil learn from this? He learns that he is an inferior being, who can-not hope to understand unless he has things explained to him by people who do!

What is the alternative? It is the weak logic of *human becoming*. In this logic, humanity is not a ready-made condition that we can attain to various degrees. It is rather what we make of it, each in our own way. For Rancière it is to start from the assumption that every human being is of equal intellect and equally capable, regard-less of age, background or any other criteria.[49] Of course everyone is different, but these differences cannot be arrayed on any scale of more or less. People are not, in other words, different in ways that are the same for all, but the same in all being dif-ferent in their own ways. Teacher and student, then, far from standing vis-à-vis one another as respectively learned and ignorant, face in the *same* direction, as *people*, each with a particular story to tell, attending and responding to one another along a journey which they undertake together but towards what outcome, no-one knows. In a word, they correspond. Rancière calls it a correspondence of wills,[50] though I would prefer to call it a correspondence of habits or *agencements*, since the volition or intentional agency of neither party should stand in the way.

What kind of pedagogy is this, in which the teacher has nothing to transmit, nothing to pass on, nor even any specific methods, protocols, rules or forms of test-ing or certification for doing so? Masschelein has a word for it: he calls it 'poor ped-agogy'.[51] It is 'the art of waiting and presenting', an invitation to lead out (*ex-ducere*), offering means to experience and to become attentive. It affords the possibility of exposure, through exercises that stretch our attention towards the real and its truth: 'not the truth about the real, but the truth that comes out of the real … in the experience'.[52] Above all, poor pedagogy is *weak*, and we are weakened by it. A strong education arms us with knowledge, allows us to shore up our defences against the vagaries of the external world, gives us immunity, and provides security and the comfort of reason. If anything troubles us, we can account for it and make it go away – or at least put it in its context. Shut up in our armour, however, and walled in by our intellectual defences, we fail to take in or respond to the reality the world presents to us. A weak education, undertaken with poor pedagogy, achieves just the opposite. It entreats us to break out of the security of our defensive posi-tions, take off our armour, and meet the world with open arms. It is a practice of disarmament. This is education in the sense of *ex-ducere*. It is about exposure rather than immunity; it renders us vulnerable rather than powerful, but by the same token, it values truth and wisdom over knowledge. Whereas strong education seeks to instil what is desired, weak education is a search for what is desirable. It is a form of longing, and insofar as it is done responsively and responsibly with others, as a duty, it is also a form of care and correspondence. But above all, it is done, and undergone, with attention.

Notes

1 I draw here on Hannah Arendt's discussion of the meaning of life (Arendt 1958: 97). See also Ingold (2015: 125–129).
2 On the distinction between listening and hearing, see Home-Cook (2015: 24–29). See also Ingold (2000: 277).
3 Dewey (1987). This work was originally published in 1934.
4 Dewey (1987: 47–58). See also Ingold (2015: 125–129).
5 Dewey (1987: 109).
6 For a discussion of the many meanings of habit, and their philosophical provenance, see Carlisle (2014).
7 Dewey (2015: 35).
8 Dewey (1987: 59).
9 Ingold (2015: 141).
10 The phenomenologist James Hatley, reflecting on the walking practice of artist Hamish Fulton, observes that 'walking, as Fulton practices it, is not the making of an experience in the sense that I own it, that I have an experience of the world, but in the sense that I undergo it, am traumatized by it … the body undergoes rather than masters the earth it walks' (Hatley 2003: 204–205).
11 See my essay 'Ways of mind-walking: reading, writing, painting', in Ingold (2011: 196–209).
12 Manning (2016: 37).
13 Manning (2016: 120).
14 'The only thing that is given to us and that *is* when there is human life is *the having to make it*, each one for himself', declared the philosopher José Ortega y Gasset, in an essay on *History as a System* composed in 1935. '*Life is a task*' (Ortega y Gasset 1961: 200, emphases in the original).
15 Dewey (1966: 68).
16 Manning (2016: 6).
17 On this, see Gell (1985: 274–275).
18 As the theatre scholar George Home-Cook (2015: 39) has observed, attention in the sense of check-up sets up distraction as its opposite, characterised by 'a loss of attention and the usurpation of the mind by the body'.
19 Ingold (2015: 133).
20 This sense of correspondence has its anthropological counterpart in classical discussions of totemism, according to which a relation of alliance between social groups maps onto an equivalent relation between natural species. Each group, then, corresponds to its totem (Lévi-Strauss 1964).
21 For further discussion of this distinction, see Ingold (2013b: 105–108).
22 'People play chess', writes anthropologist Robert Desjarlais of his experience at the board, 'but it could also be said that the game plays them… While playing chess you can be carried along by the formal flow of the game… Social life proceeds in much the same way' (Desjarlais 2011: 16).
23 Biesta (2006: 64–65); see also Lingis (1994: 130–131).

24 Ingold (2005: 171).
25 Masschelein and Simons (2013: 47).
26 Dewey (1987: 80).
27 Dewey (1966: 51).
28 Masschelein (2010a: 276–277).
29 Masschelein (2010a: 276).
30 Masschelein (2010b: 44, 50).
31 Masschelein (2010a: 278).
32 Masschelein (2010a: 282).
33 Masschelein (2010a: 278).
34 Gibson's theory is set out in its most comprehensive form in *The Ecological Approach to Visual Perception* (1979). On the 'path of observation', see Gibson (1979: 197), also Ingold (2000: 226–228, 238–240).
35 Ingold (2001: 142).
36 Gibson (1979: 254); see also Ingold (2001).
37 Ingold (2015: 138–142).
38 Dewey (1987: 62).
39 Masschelein (2010a: 282).
40 Ingold (2015: 136).
41 Although this declaration is commonly attributed to Yeats (e.g., Biesta 2013: 1), evidence to support this attribution has proved elusive. The most likely source seems to have been the Graeco-Roman author Plutarch. In his essay, 'On listening', Plutarch wrote: 'the correct analogy for the mind is not a vessel that needs filling, but wood that needs igniting' (Plutarch 1992: 50).
42 Biesta (2013: 17).
43 On this distinction, see Ingold (2013a: 6–9).
44 Biesta (2013: 1).
45 Wieman (1961: 63–66). For further discussion of Wieman's ideas, see Ingold (2014a).
46 Biesta (2013: 23).
47 Rancière (1991: 6).
48 Rancière (1991: 3).
49 Rancière (1991: 101).
50 Rancière (1991: 13).
51 Masschelein (2010b).
52 Masschelein (2010a: 283–285).

3
EDUCATION IN THE MINOR KEY

The undercommons

I have been concerned, in the last chapter, to draw a distinction between the strong sense of education as the delivery of grand, powerful statements that provide a kind of founding charter for civilisation-as-we-know-it, and a weak sense as the hesitant overflowings or deviations that pull us out of certainty, out of our defensive positions and standpoints – that disarm us. This, as Masschelein has shown us, is how *educare* differs from *ex-ducere*. However the distinction is really just one instance of a more general contrast between what philosopher Gilles Deleuze and psychoanalyst Félix Guattari distinguish as the sciences of the 'major' and the 'minor'.[1] Thus we could say of an education that leads out, through exposure rather than indoctrination, that it is conducted in the minor key. The musical analogy is apt, for the difference between major and minor modes is precisely that while the major is confident, assertive and affirmative, the minor is anxious, unsettling and inquisitive. The major is a carrier of light, whereas the minor is often felt to be dark in tone. For those who believe in enlightenment, darkness is something to be expelled. The idea of an education into darkness would sound, to them, at best like a contradiction in terms, at worst like a recipe for decline and despair. But they are the victors in contests over knowledge: people of Culture rather than people in cultures; scientists rather than traditional folk; adults rather than children. And where there are victors there are also vanquished, for whom the conquerors' enlightenment is experienced as oppression, subjugation or the production of ignorance. My contention, in this chapter, is that only an education that admits of variations in the minor key can afford a freedom that is real rather than illusory, and lead us out of structures of authority that are manifestly unsustainable. It is not that such education condemns us to the darkness of an unlit cave so much as that it alone enables us to carry on, to keep life going, and to offer new beginnings for generations to come.[2]

To begin, let me return to what Dewey called 'communication', for which I have substituted the term 'commoning'. To common, in this sense, is not to regress to a set of baseline attributes with which all participants are endowed to begin with. It rather entails an attentive stretch whereby every participant casts their experience forward in ways that can answer to the experience of others, and they likewise, so as to achieve a correspondence that goes beyond what any of them could have imagined at the outset, and that in turn allows them to carry on their lives together. This casting forward – or what I have called 'longing' – is not directed to a target. It has no predetermined aims or objectives. Its longed-for ends are as yet undefined and undefinable, beyond the horizons of conceptualisation, and for that very reason they remain open to all. The excess, in longing, of undergoing over doing allows those who have nothing in common nevertheless to welcome each other's presence, to attend and respond to one another and, in so doing, to fashion a community of relations. By what term, then, should we know the region in which commoning goes on? Stefano Harney and Fred Moten – the one a theorist of education, the other a literary scholar – call it the 'undercommons'.[3]

It is always there, the undercommons, even if we rarely acknowledge its existence. And being there, it continually animates or enlivens a world that would otherwise be bound to predetermined motions. Under*commoning*, thus conceived, is the very antithesis of the under*standing* that is often taken as a precondition for social civility and as the primary goal of education. With understanding, knowledge pre-empts attention. As we saw in the last chapter, understanding establishes a basis upon which everyone and everything can be put in position. It lays a ground of certain knowledge, literally a substrate to stand on. Sharing a common standpoint, we can close up, secure in our foundations. Understanding is in the major key. But undercommoning is in the minor. It pulls everyone and everything out of position, out of any standpoint they may have held. The undercommons is subject to tremors; it shakes things up. This is rather like the feeling you get when, walking in the terrain, awareness dawns that you have lost your way. Somewhere you have veered from the path; everything seems strangely out of joint. The ground across which you previously strode with such confidence now offers insecure footing.[4] You are at risk, even exposed. But at the same time, you attend as never before, as every sound, every flicker of light and every feeling are magnified in intensity. It is in the insecurity of undercommoning, and not the security of understanding, that we truly open to one another and to the world.

Now this kind of magnification, as Erin Manning has shown, is characteristic of the perceptual experience of those who – in the language of mainstream psychiatry – would be diagnosed as autistic.[5] Classically defined as a condition of withdrawal, stemming from the lack or absence of normal abilities to interact with others, Manning provides ample testimony, supported by the writings of autistics themselves, that it is just the opposite. What for most of us comes to the foreground only in moments of radical uncertainty – such as when, out walking, we are lost – is for autistic people a chronic condition. Theirs is not a closure so much as an openness which, on occasion, can become unbearable. Withdrawal, insofar as it occurs, is a defensive reaction to what can be an overwhelming surge of sensory stimulation, as we might hold our hands to our ears in response to excessive noise or shield our eyes from the light. As Manning observes, this can make autistics seem disengaged or even distracted when in truth 'they are lingering in the true fullness of attention, lured by infinite complexity'.[6] In the last chapter I distinguished two senses of distraction by way of their opposition to alternative accounts of attention, framed respectively by the principles of volition and habit. In one sense – the opposite of the stop-and-check – distraction signifies a loss of mental focus; in the other – the opposite of responsive accompaniment – it signifies a deviation in the line of attention. In the case of autistics, what we take for the former is in truth the latter: it is the distraction of the lure, in which a super-engaged attention is pulled in so many ways at once as to be rendered immobile. It is because we confuse the two that we are so apt to diagnose autistic distraction as a deficit in attention.

Autistics linger, according to Manning, precisely in the region that the rest of us pass through so quickly that we scarcely even notice, unless of course we lose our way. We take a short cut into form, seeing ourselves surrounded by people and objects that we can readily categorise. We know who and what they are. And only then, from the security of our respective positions – like allegorical chess-players – do we begin to interact with them. Closure is the default position, from which we attribute intentions, motives and standpoints to others.[7] But they, autistics, are always *edging into form*, abiding in the midst of things where nothing is yet settled, placing in the foreground the welling of ever-varying experience before it succumbs to partition and categorisation. They are already attending and responding to the phenomenal world, even before any possibility of formal identification and interaction can arise. 'There is an important time-lapse', as Manning puts it, 'between the direct perception of the emergent ecology and the actual taking-form of the objects and subjects in its midst'.[8] In autistic perception, it is as though this lapse were experienced in slow motion. Yet autistic perception, Manning also insists, 'does not belong exclusively to autistics'.[9] It is common to infants, whose lively awareness has still to be curtailed by adult disciplinary oppression, and to the ways of being of indigenous people whom anthropologists have classically categorised as 'animists'. Theirs is a world of movement and becoming, of incipience or continuous birth, in which everything and everyone is forever on the verge of revealing itself for what it is or for who they are.

Indeed to the extent that the spark of attention has not been fully extinguished, such that life can go on, this kind of perception is common to all of us, albeit suppressed by the majoritarian privileging of final forms. It is common to all of us because, like it or not, we are inhabitants of the undercommons before we can ever find our feet in solid understanding. This is the region of autistic lingering, of the awakenings of infancy and of animic world-forming, and it is alive with what Manning calls 'minor gestures', those little disturbances or distractions where things veer off course, opening experience to potential variation. As we saw in Chapter 1, there can be no commoning without variation. The minor gesture is the source of variation that makes commoning possible. Even if overshadowed by the grand gestures – the assertions, the categorisations, the explications – of the major, the minor gesture is always there, always nudging from behind the scenes. And the question Manning poses in a recent book, which adopts the minor gesture as its title, is this: what if we were to take the experience of autism (or of infancy, or animism) as a starting point for inquiry, rather than as an abnormality, or as a condition to be grown out of or to be superseded by reason? What if we were to begin not with the 'able-bodied-ness' of a complete, fully-armed and immunised being, but with the lively openness of body to world characteristic of autistics, infants and animists?

Perhaps the opposite of 'able-bodied' should not be 'disabled' but 'enlivened'. The enlivened body may be at risk, and vulnerable to exposure, but it is at least alive to the world. Where the able body of the self-sufficient, volitional agent is set to work in the realisation of its intentions, the enlivened body is always in the midst of 'doing undergoing', of calling being to life, or what Manning calls 'life-living'.[10] It is animate. What, then, if we were to start with the edging into form, the welling of experience, the ecology of attention, the phenomenology of direct perception, of animate being? In a word, what if we were to set out in the minor key? How could we use this to challenge the hegemonic doctrines of the major? What are the implications of such a challenge for the ways we think about education, study and the school, teaching and learning, and the freedoms they both depend upon and exemplify? These are the questions I address in this chapter. And my reading of Manning's book, *The Minor Gesture*, has inspired me to write it.

The major and the minor

There are two kinds of science, say Deleuze and Guattari.[11] One plots the determined motions of particulate bodies in a space that can be divided, reckoned and apportioned. This is major science, with which we are all too familiar from what we have been taught at school. We take it for granted, in this science, that solidity is primordial, fluidity derivative; that identity and constancy come before difference and variation; that movement is the rectilinear transposition of a body from point to point; that complexity can be factored out by way of the quantitative computation of its elements. Minor science, always an undercurrent to the major and without which it could not exist, is the opposite in every respect. It begins with fluidity and sees, in things that seem to us fixed in form and constitution, only the outlines or envelopes of perpetual movement. In so doing it posits variation, heterogeneity and becoming before constancy, homogeneity and being. With minor science, movement is not the transposition but the generation of form, but only insofar as the movement itself moves: in that it veers or curves from the straight line defined as the shortest distance between points. Its relations are topological, not statistical; its complexity non-computable. And its space – here folded and crumpled, there stretched and taut – cannot be reckoned or divided. In the terms of Deleuze and Guattari, it is smooth rather than striated.[12] One can consider it neither in its magnitude or extension, nor in its capacity for arithmetic multiplication or division, but only in its potential for distortion, transformation or metamorphosis.

Contemporary cosmologists, determined to defend the authority of the major against the intrusions of the minor, have been falling over themselves in their attempts to explain how in the convolutions of the universe, space itself can bend by determinate amounts and time pass at different speeds, landing themselves in contradictions famously parodied by the artist Marcel Duchamp, when in *Three Standard Stoppages* he dropped three pieces of string of exactly one metre in length, from a height of one metre, onto three stretched canvases. The curves and inflections of the fallen strings, each caught in the act of an aerial twist and tumble, tease us with the question: 'Where is your metre now?' No one string can be the measure of them all. How can we measure the variations of a string if the very operation of measurement requires us to straighten it – thus eliminating all the variation? Try it yourself: every piece of string, as it falls, lands in its own singular way, never straight, at every point along its length veering slightly off course. The only way to measure such a piece is to join with it, to retrace its length, or in a word, to *follow* it. Measuring, then, is following; the metre not pegged to an absolute value but performed in the gesture of the trace. To take the measure of things, in minor science, is not to plot a series of points and connect them up in a higher order of relation. One goes not from facts 'on the ground' to theories, by *in*-duction, nor conversely from theories to facts by a reverse process of *de*-duction, but rather along the sensible path of a continuous variation, that is by *ex*-duction. One is led out along the way.

Every such way, according to Deleuze and Guattari, is a problem rather than a theorem.[13] The theorem is rational, the problem affective. And the thing about real problems is that far from closing in on a solution, they afford an opening. False problems already contain their solutions, hidden inside them, and the challenge is to find them. The jigsaw puzzle, the Rubik's cube, the crossword: all have their one correct answer, and their resolution can in principle and with practice be speeded up to the point at which they take no time at all. But real problems have no solutions. They must be given time – a time that is given over to what Manning calls 'patient experimentation'.[14] This is not the patience of the major scientist who, ratchet-like, would go back over the same procedure, again and again, in order to verify his results. The aim in patient experimentation is not to test a preconceived hypothesis but to open a path and follow wherever it may take you. It is not so much iterative as itinerant; a journey undertaken rather than a cycle of returns on a fixed point. It works more by intuition than by reason; opening from within rather than penetrating from without. It is prospective rather than retroactive, improvisatory rather than prescriptive, speculative rather than confirmatory. The patience of experimentation, in this sense, lies in the dynamics of attention, and in the endurance of waiting. We have to allow things to come into presence, in their own time: they cannot be forced.

Consider for example the path made by walking. The path is a real problem: it challenges us to follow, but in following we do not solve the problem but continually answer to it. That is to say, we correspond with it. The path offers a way of carrying on and being carried, along which we have to feel our way forward, each footfall taking us no closer to any final solution but each nevertheless heralding a new beginning. One problem, as we say, leads to another. And every variable step, as we walk together in the undercommons, is a minor gesture. In walking as in any other movement of habit, an undefinable longing that wells up in attention and draws us out along the path eventually matures into a precisely directed and skilfully executed manoeuvre: the step. Thus does submission give way to mastery, as breathing in to breathing out.[15] For Manning, this makes the movement *decisional* rather than volitional.[16] The decision literally entails a cut, but it is a cut of a particular kind. One way to get at its particularity is by comparing the way we might cut timber: across the grain with a saw versus along the grain with an axe. The saw, cutting transversally, delivers an external determination. I have measured up the timber, and have wilfully decided where to cut in order to divide it into blocks of the desired lengths. The wood is mere matter in my hands, to be shaped to my specification, and as I cut, it is reduced to homogeneous pulp beneath the blade. With the axe, by contrast, I enter into the grain, opening up the wood from the inside along a fibrous line that I have not drawn myself but which has been incorporated into the timber during a history of growth, when it was part of a living tree. 'It is a question of surrendering to the wood', say Deleuze and Guattari, 'then following where it leads'.[17]

In woodcutting the decision emerges from this correspondence of timber and metal, and from the forces pent up in each as they strike up an engagement. It is a decision taken in the cutting, not in advance of it, and it alters the course of the event, as Manning puts it, '*in the event*'.[18] In so doing it introduces a variation, not in the movement itself, but *in the way movement moves*. This is what Manning calls an 'inflection'. The point of inflection marks the transition from submission to mastery, or from longing to manoeuvre, where 'a vague incipiency becomes a directionality'.[19] And to attend to it means perceiving movement's differentials: in the splitting of timber or the variable gait of the walker, but equally in the rising or falling of the melodic line in singing or in the ductus of handwriting. Every decisional cut – be it in woodwork, walking, singing or writing – entails a differential in the way of movement-moving that eventually takes it in this direction or in that. This is what skill is about: not imposing exterior form on compliant matter but finding the grain of things and bending it to an evolving purpose.[20] It is no accident that the word 'skill' has its roots in the Middle Low German *schillen*, 'to make a difference', and in the Old Norse *skilja*, 'to divide, separate, distinguish, decide'; nor that it shares an etymological affinity with the word 'shell', a casing that is opened up by splitting or cleaving along the grain. The minor gesture cleaves the event from within. It is, in short, a mode of what I shall call 'interstitial differentiation'.[21]

The freedom of habit

Let me return once again to the two senses of attention introduced in Chapter 2, founded respectively in the principles of volition and habit. In the first sense, of stop-and-check, attention interrupts movement in order to establish a transverse relation between subject and object, mind and world. In the second sense, of responsive accompaniment, attention follows the animate movements with which it is resonantly coupled: it is a go-along, not transverse but longitudinal. From Masschelein, we have already learned how the road of attention, taken in this latter sense, cuts a way through the transverse links posited by an attention of the former kind. As should now be evident, this distinction between the transverse and the longitudinal is precisely equivalent to the one drawn above, between the major and the minor. The two keys are orthogonal to one another. It is the claim of the major that we orchestrate and direct our actions from without; that for each and every move we make we have taken a decision of our own volition and proceed to act upon it. Such claims, however, typically belong to the way we explain our deeds in retrospect, that is, by what Manning calls a 'backgridding' onto events that have already taken place.[22] We might feel that we have acted of our own accord, as though our intentional agency were the cause and the action the effect, but the feeling of volition should not be confused with volition itself. The truth is that it is no more possible for us to stand outside our actions and assume total control from the start than it is to separate, in experience, what we do from what we undergo. In practice, decisions emerge in the doing, where the doer remains inside the deed. Here, the act emerges from within the field of attention as an incipient movement, barely felt at first, matures into a firm sense of direction. This is to acknowledge the generative force of the minor.

Does this acknowledgement imply that we are any less free than we thought? Not at all. I want to argue, to the contrary, that the principle of volition grants only an illusory freedom, and that real freedom is to be found in the principle of habit. This is not a question of which affords more freedom, habit or volition? It is a question of the *kind* of freedom that is at stake. To find an answer, let us rejoin the walker on the path. What kind of freedom does he enjoy? It is not a freedom he owns, as an individual, to use as he pleases. For he is bound to submit to the path, and to follow where it leads. But nor is he subject to an external determination, as are the inmates of a maze who, faced with multiple options at every turn, are nevertheless walled in on all sides.[23] The maze is a puzzle that already contains its solution: it is a false problem. And likewise the freedom it affords is a false freedom. Just as false problems are defined by their solutions, false freedoms are defined by their objectives. The maze is a set-up, and its inmates, thinking themselves free, are in fact already imprisoned. False freedom ends in the objectives that necessity places before it. The path made by walking, however, though it may vary in intensity, always carries on, always overshoots its objectives, *and therein lies its freedom*. This is not an elective freedom, to choose between a finite spread of options or – as in the formal definition of economics – to allocate scarce means to alternative ends. It is rather a freedom to improvise, to find a way as you go along in response to environmental variations. Rather than a choice among ends, the path affords perpetual beginning; rather than the freedom to take a stand, it affords movement; rather than the freedom to exchange and interact, it affords growth and correspondence.

In short, just as the path made by walking is a real problem, so its freedom is a real freedom. Critically, real freedom is not constituted by its opposition to the necessity of external determination. The paradox of false freedom, as philosopher Roberto Esposito has observed, is that it is inexorably dragged 'toward a destined outcome, toward its very negation'.[24] Such freedom must always define itself *against* necessity. You may be free to pursue your chosen objectives, but whence came these objectives? The much-vaunted 'free will' of the human subject would amount to no more than aimless vibration, within the bounds of pre-existing structural determinations, were it not underwritten by some prior purpose. Perhaps this purpose, too, has arisen by a free act of will, itself underwritten by a purpose that has originated likewise. But this regressive accounting, however far we might attempt to take it – and it could, in principle, recede to infinity – can never exhaust the experience of the living, creative being. And it is in the excess of experience over action, in the encompassment of doing within undergoing – or in short, in our *dwelling in habit* – that the locus of real freedom resides. Such freedom, writes Esposito, 'must be understood not as something that one has but as something that one is', not the exclusive preserve of our essential humanity but the release of human being into existence, into life.[25] Thus the freedom of the path is not a negative – it is not anti-necessity – but a positive affirmation of life, growth and movement. Life has no destined outcome save further life; growth, no outcome save further growth; movement, no outcome save further movement. Where volitional freedom is end-directed, the freedom of habit, as Esposito puts it, is 'pure beginning'.[26]

This carries the crucial corollary, moreover, that freedom and necessity must go hand-in-hand. They are not opposed but co-dependent. Indeed the principle of their co-dependence is already familiar to us, for it is the same principle that makes variation a condition of commoning, and vice versa. Esposito finds the principle lurking in the very etymology of the words 'freedom' and 'liberty', the one having its roots in Sanskrit *frya* (whence 'free', 'friend'), the other in Indo-European *leuth* or *leudh* (whence 'love', 'life', in German *lieb*). In its originary sense, he concludes, freedom has nothing to do with the removal of impediment or constraint. It rather 'carries a powerfully affirmative sense that is altogether political, biological and physical, and which recalls an expansion, blossoming, or common growth, or a growth that brings together'.[27] Now Esposito does not hazard an etymology of necessity, but had he done so, he would likely have reached much the same conclusion. For the word is compounded from Latin *nectere* ('to bind', possibly from Indo-European *noc*, whence 'knot' and 'nexus') and *esse* ('to be'). Necessity binds lives in love and friendship – that is, in liberty and freedom. Perhaps there is a distinction to be made between real and false necessity, just as there is between real and false freedom. False necessity joins things *up*, like the words of a sentence or the parts of a machine, into an articulated structure. In a fully connected structure, in which everything is joined up, nothing could live or grow. Real necessity, by contrast, means joining *with*, as in the correspondence of lives, and indeed of generations, that go along together, as do young and old, children and their parents, pupils and their teachers. This is not a rigid necessity that admits of freedom only in the choice of different combinatorial possibilities, but a supple necessity born of commitment and attention to others and the ways they want to go.[28]

This is the point at which to return to the notion of *agencement*, which I introduced in the last chapter – following Manning – to denote the 'doing undergoing' of habit. By contrast to the agency of the volitional subject, I take *agencement* to refer to the way in which the 'I' of habit is continually engendered in the wake of action, more as question than assertion. For Manning, *agencement* is equivalent to the decisional process that I have here called interstitial differentiation, opening up the 'cleave of the event' from within. It is, in her definition, 'the directed intensity of a compositional movement that alters the field of experience'.[29] In French the word is the gerund of the verb *agencer*, which might be rendered in English, albeit awkwardly, as 'to agence', hence 'agencing'. Yet in its primary meaning, *agencer* suggests something altogether different, which implies neither cleaving, nor differentiation, nor even generation. It rather means to fit together parts that bear only an external relation to one another in order to make a coherent whole: as, for example, when you build a model from a construction kit. In a word, it is to assemble. An *agencement*, then, is quite simply an assembly. It is this double meaning of *agencement*, referring at once to a process of interstitial differentiation and exterior assembly, of correspondence and articulation, joining *with* and joining *up*, that has made the term so difficult to translate, but also so rich in semantic potential.

Deleuze and Guattari make full use of this potential in co-opting *agencement* as the fulcrum around which to assemble the sprawling meditations that make up their co-written volume, *A Thousand Plateaus*. In their hands, it works to pull things apart – or to free them up – from the determinations of their exterior articulation, precisely in order that their constituent materials may be released into the compositional movement of their affective correspondence. A book, they say, is an *agencement* in this sense. A book, *their* book, 'has neither object nor subject; it is made of variously formed matters … We will never ask what a book means…; we will not look for anything to understand it. We will ask what it functions with.'[30] Deleuze and Guattari are pleading with us, their readers, not to treat the book as a complete artefact, contained within its covers, to be analysed and interpreted. They want us to read the book as they wrote it, and in so doing to weave our thinking with theirs – to correspond with them – in a journey without end, one that we undertake together. Writing, for them, is like walking: it is 'an experimentation in contact with the real',[31] an improvisatory movement that is at every moment responsive to the tendencies of things. Here every word, like every step, is a minor gesture, a moment of exposure. What *agencement* does, then, is effect a modulation from the major to the minor key.

The freedom opened up by this move, Manning writes, 'affects us, moves us, directs us, *but it does not belong to us*'.[32] It belongs neither singly, as an exclusive entitlement, nor in common, to some sort of collectivity characterised by the pre-possession of a common identity. It belongs rather – in Manning's words – to a 'collectivity alive with difference'.[33] This is the community (*com-munus*) – in the sense already encountered in Chapter 1 – of those with something to give because they have nothing in common. It is the undercommons. Thus the freedom to which I belong (as opposed to the freedom that belongs to me), and by which I am possessed, is the freedom of the undercommons. Such freedom is a property not of individual minds, singly or collectively, but of an ecology of relations. But so too is the necessity with which it corresponds. Both real freedom and real necessity are exemplified in the minor gestures through which lives are lived together in the undercommons. Here, freedom *falls* to us as a task – we *owe* it rather than *own* it – and in its fulfilment we discharge our debt to others, not as an obligation but as a duty. We are at once free and duty-bound to respond to others. This, as we have seen, is how we bring others into presence, and care for them. There can be no freedom, in this sense, without responsibility, and without care. That, finally, is what it means to dwell in the freedom of habit.

On what it means to study

In Ancient Greece, school (*scholè*) was designated as free time.[34] To today's students and their teachers this sounds strange if not contradictory. Surely, time in school is just the opposite of free: it is time during which students are tied to an institutionalised regime of behavioural and disciplinary constraint, and teachers to the precisely scheduled delivery of a prescribed curriculum. Freedom signifies leisure, time off; those intervals when institutional constraints are relaxed and private desires can take precedence. But in his reflections on the original meaning of education, Masschelein explains that school-time was free, in Greek Antiquity, in quite another sense. *Scholè*, as he puts it, meant 'time without destination and without aim or end'.[35] It was free because while attending school, pupils could temporarily set aside, or hold in abeyance, the normative expectations and hierarchies of status that regulated their lives in society. In this liminal, in-between space they could join with their teachers in a community of equals, but one in which each is different, and each has something to give. The purpose of school was not to furnish every child with a destiny in life and the means to fulfil it, in the form of a given identity with its particular ways of speaking, acting and thinking. Quite the reverse: it was to un-destine, to suspend the trappings of social order, to detach means from ends – words from meanings, property from use, acts from intentions, thinking from thoughts – so as to set them free, bring them into presence in the here-and-now, and place them at the disposal of all. Here, in school, nothing is what it was, or what it yet will be. And as an architect of *scholè*, the educator or teacher, according to Masschelein, 'is one who un-finishes, who undoes the appropriation and destination of time'.[36] He or she is not so much a custodian of ends as a catalyst of beginnings, whose task it is to restore both memory and imagination to the temporal stretch of life.

Education in this sense is a form of longing, a practice of care, a way of doing undergoing, and its freedom is the freedom of habit. What Masschelein has characterised, under the rubric of *scholè*, is of course none other than the undercommons: 'a field of relations', as Manning describes it, 'fabulated at the interstices of the now and the not-yet'.[37] It is a field alive with minor gestures, in which false problems can be set aside for real ones – 'open problems that bring us together in the mode of active inquiry'.[38] These are problems that do not yield to answers but only to further problems, further encounters, further openings. That is why proper study can never be the application of method. For method, aligned to the major, 'seeks to capture the minor gesture'.[39] Converting questions into results, into answers, method brings study to a standstill, puts an end to it. What keeps it going, to the contrary, is patient experimentation. Patient study is critical, but it is not critique. It has no subject or object. It does not start with the already-thought, or triangulate between fixed positions or standpoints. 'Where I stand', for Manning, is – like its complement, the 'object of study' – the least interesting of questions: the question that stops study in its tracks, aligning it to disciplinary method and institutional power.[40] For study to carry on, critical thinking must overtake self-conscious critique: study, says Manning, 'delights in the activation of the as-yet-unthought'.[41] In study, thinking always exceeds conceptualisation; that's what makes it speculative. The practices of study, patiently experimental, always open to excess, untethered to a stand, pragmatically speculative, are 'entrenched in their own process of making-time', and yet – in the suspension of that time, in their holding in abeyance the demands of society, its appropriations of the past and its projects for the future – they 'remain untimely'.[42] Study in the undercommons, Manning concludes, 'brings past and future into a mobile coexistence'.[43]

A number of consequences follow from this view of study, and I want to focus on just three of them. The first is that study cannot be done on one's own. The idea of 'independent study', as something carried on in isolation, is simply untenable. One is never alone. 'Study is what you do with other people', says Moten, in an interview with social theorist Stevphen Shukaitis. 'It's talking and walking around with other people, working, dancing, suffering, some irreducible convergence of all three.'[44] And Harney, his co-author, agrees:

> I've been thinking more and more of study as something not where everybody dissolves into the student, but where people sort of take turns doing things for each other or for the others, and where you allow yourself to be possessed by others as they do something. That also is a kind of dispossession of what you might otherwise have been holding onto, and that possession is released in a certain way voluntarily, and then some other possession occurs by others.[45]

This mutual dispossession – this offering to others of what one has, or even of what one *is* – is tantamount, in our terms, to the process of commoning. In this, whatever knowledge and experience participants might bring to the process – be it in the guise of a written text, a mathematical formula or a manual gesture – must be unshackled from the contexts in which it finds use and significance in the prevailing social order, and offered up just as it is. It must be *made public*, there for all to see or hear, and to make of it what they will. As Masschelein and Simons put it, in their defence of the school as a site of study, the thing must be 'unhanded and placed on the table'.[46] School, for Masschelein and Simons, is where persons gather around the table, and attend to the things placed there. And attending to things for what they are, not as a means to ends, is what Masschelein and Simons call 'study'. For them, study lies not in the appropriation of knowledge but in its disappropriation, its defamiliarisation and deprivatisation. Suspended from use, perhaps by people of the older generation, it is *not yet* appropriated by those of the younger. This is what makes it possible for every generation to begin afresh, to experience themselves as a *new* generation.[47]

The second consequence of this view of study is that it is not intermediate but in-between.[48] By 'intermediate' I mean a stage of transition from one state to another: from past to present, from childhood to adulthood, from ignorance to knowledge. The direction of travel is from here to there, and the student – halfway across – never ceases to be conscious of where he has come from and where he is going. This is what it means to study in the major key. The minor, however, irrupts into this linear sequence, and pours through the breach as a river through a burst dam. In his reflections on upbringing in *The Troubadour of Knowledge*, Michel Serres has resort to just such an image when he compares himself to a swimmer, breasting the current of a swift river. Here, in the midstream, he enters a second river unknown to those left standing on the banks: to friends and family, to officialdom, to the majority. This second river, after a while, no longer has any right bank or left bank; it affords no way back to dry land or immediate prospect of arrival on the other side, no anticipated foothold in solidity. Instead, the swimmer is borne headlong by a current that has no point of origin or final destination, in a direction orthogonal to the line connecting the banks on either side. 'The real passage', Serres declares, 'occurs in the middle'.[49] This is the in-between. It is, in French, a *milieu* (literally, 'middle-place'), a word that English has readily borrowed, perhaps for want of a better alternative. The remarkable thing about the milieu, however, is that while for the majority it exists only as the finest line between here and there – a line without thickness or dimension; indeed a geometrical abstraction – in the experience of the swimmer as he enters the second river it explodes into an entire cosmos that envelops and swallows him at its heart.[50] The imperceptible midline unfolds into a universe. And that, suggest Masschelein and Simons, is just how we should imagine the school. It is an almost invisible, in-between place, a milieu. From the outside it seems enclosed, even claustrophobic. But for those who enter in, it opens up to reveal a world.[51]

The student, diving into the milieu, must however leave his belongings behind. This is the third entailment of study in the minor key, and again the *scholè* of Greek antiquity offers a model. The pupil was originally defined as an orphan, someone with no family. In school, the child is temporarily turned into a pupil by being stripped of his familial connections. This was the task of the pedagogue, usually a household slave who literally walked the child from home to school but left him at the gates, playing no part in what went on within. Is it so different today? Daniel Pennac, writing in *School Blues* of his experience of teaching 'difficult' students in suburban districts of France, speaks of the importance of allowing students to detach themselves, if only for some hours every day, from a past that already defines them as deficient, and from a future devoid of prospects. He sees them coming to school, each wrapped like an onion in layer after layer of fear, worry, bitterness and anger: 'Look, here they come, their bodies in the process of becoming and their families in their rucksacks. The lesson can't really begin until the burden has been laid down and the onion peeled.'[52] Once having shed their skins, they can embark on a process of renewal. Past and future are set aside, while they are drawn into what Pennac calls the 'present indicative'.[53] This is the suspended present of the *here-and-now* that nevertheless remains untimely, as Mannning says, in its slide into the minor key.[54] But being collectively present, both here and now, means not only that you are present to others. They are also present to you. They, too, are lifted from the positions and categorisations into which they have been consigned by the majority, freed up from the ends to which they are customarily deployed, and brought to our attention not as *objects* of regard but as animate *things* in their own right, to which we are bound to respond. It is at this moment, say Masschelein and Simons, 'that things – detached from private uses and positions – become "real"'.[55] They act, they speak to us directly, make us think: not just *about* them but *with* them. They become part of our world, as we are of theirs. We care for them, as they for us. That is what it means to study.

From explanation to feeling

Let us take a step back to reassert the majority position. Study, in the major key, is a rigorous and methodical endeavour of knowledge acquisition. Its purpose is to lay the foundations for future understanding. It has a beginning and an end point. At the beginning, the student lacks knowledge, but by the end she has come into possession of it. But as we saw in Chapter 1, 'acquisition' can be read in two opposed senses, and only one of these qualifies as study. This is the sense attributed to science and civilisation: the progressive acquisition of knowledge through empirical inquiry and rational analysis. Study in this sense is active, it is what we do, it frames and justifies the tests we undergo, and it serves to raise us up from ignorance to enlightenment. But this sense precipitates its opposite: namely, acquisition as the mere absorption of traditional ways by means of the allegedly inferior mechanism of imitation. That is how folk in other cultures are supposed to learn, 'naturally' and without effort, and it is a way of learning that we often attribute to the very young of our own social circles. Compare, for example, how we tend to describe the learning, on the one hand, by infants of their mother tongue, and on the other hand, by schoolchildren of languages other than their own. We would not hesitate to describe the schoolchild as a student of a foreign language. Yet it seems almost perverse to describe the infant as a student of her mother tongue. The nursery, surely, is not a place of study, unless you happen to be there as a researcher into early child development. What does this difference say about mainstream attitudes to education? What if, instead, we were to think of the infant as a student par excellence?

It is this latter question that Rancière takes as a point of departure, in his critical exploration of the emancipatory potential of education.[56] In Chapter 2 we learned from Rancière how education in the strong sense – that is, in the major key – while

promising emancipation, actually reproduces the perception of a fundamental inequality of intelligence between those tasked as pedagogues, with the explication of
knowledge, and those committed as students, to having it explained to them. Turning convention on its head, Rancière argues that it is not the ignorant who need
explicators, in order that they may eventually assume the mantle of civilisation, but
rather the explicators who need the ignorant, and indeed constitute them as such, in
order that they may demonstrate their acquired mastery. Strong education, far from
lifting every generation up, is a put-down that each inflicts, in turn, on its successors.
It amounts, in Rancière's words, not to enlightened understanding but to 'enforced
stultification'.[57] Why, he wonders, should students need to have things explained to
them at all? Given the requisite materials, and an incentive to study them together,
are they not intelligent enough to work things out for themselves? And once having done so, does this not bring about a comprehension more profound than could
ever be achieved by even the most powerful methods of explication?

This, after all, is precisely how children, in infancy, learn their mother tongue.
Anyone who has brought up a child knows very well that language does not come
as a ready-made structure that has only to be inserted into an infantile mind innately
pre-programmed to receive it, and that its acquisition – involving a huge amount of
patient experimentation, founded in attention and responsiveness, care and longing –
is an open-ended process of rediscovery. Indeed there is every reason to describe
this process as one of education, and the infant as a student, in the weak sense set
out in the foregoing paragraphs. And if children can so readily achieve fluency in
their mother tongue, why should we not allow that they can achieve mastery in
other fields with the same intelligence, and in much the same way? Yet everything
in society proceeds as if it were otherwise, as though the child, on commencing formal education, could no longer depend upon the same intelligence that has served
so well until then. It is as if an opacity has set in – an opacity that comes with the
very idea of *understanding*. It is this idea that creates a deficit, and puts the child at
a loss. 'The child who is *explained to*', Rancière writes, 'will devote his intelligence
to the work of grieving: … to understanding that he doesn't understand unless he
is explained to'.[58] All the advances that go into making things understood – the
perfection of teaching methods, the simplification of complex arguments, the explication of explications – turn out only to exacerbate the condition of stultification.

What's the alternative? We all know things that have never been explained to
us, things that may even be inexplicable. We depend on this knowledge at every
moment of our lives for the accomplishment of practical tasks. It is knowledge
that has grown in us in the practice of habit, through the experiential enactments
of doing undergoing, yet which is so deeply ingrained in our person as to remain
out of reach of explication and analysis. The philosopher Michael Polanyi called
it 'tacit knowledge'.[59] What is available for explication, Polanyi thought, is but a
pinnacle compared to the immensity of the tacit domain that lies beneath. But his
was nevertheless a majoritarian position which, in setting the tacit in diametrical
opposition to the explicit, forces the knowledge and intelligence of the formally
uneducated underground, into subterranean levels of consciousness. Even Manning

succumbs to the temptation to relegate knowledge born of habit to the realm of the sub-conscious, 'beneath the words'.[60] Other theorists, enamoured of the concept of embodiment, have allowed it to sink even further, into the dark recesses of unthinking bodily automatism, where habit becomes *habitus*.[61] But the minor no more runs beneath the major than does a river beneath its banks. It is not beneath but amidst; its domain opens out from middle-place (*milieu*) to encompass the world. The milieu is not a concealed deposit; it is an opening to feeling – to what Harney and Moten, in their account of the undercommons, call the 'feel for feeling others feeling you', or 'hapticality'.[62] It runs in a dimension orthogonal to the major, not diametrical to it. To call this haptic dimension 'tacit' is a misnomer. If anything stops up knowledge and commits it to silence, it is the logic of explication.

Explication, for Polanyi, meant putting things into words, in speech or writing, or into equivalent symbols, as in a mathematical formula. This, he thought, entails the twin operations of specification and articulation. To specify means to pin things down to fixed coordinates of reference; to articulate means to join them up into a complete structure. Thus we specify when we plot dots on a graph, enter values in an equation, or type words on a page; we articulate when we join them up: dots with lines, values with plus or minus signs, words with spaces. The sentence of type – structured through and through, book-ended by a capital and a full stop – is the quintessence of literate articulation. Like the prisoner in his cell, also sentenced to a fixed term, its words are incarcerated, condemned to silence and immobility. Specification and articulation, the keys to logical explanation, lock the doors to feeling.[63]

What then escapes? Does the unspecifiable part of knowledge – what Polanyi described as 'the residue left unsaid by defective articulation'[64] – fall through the cracks into mute and illiterate incoherence? Or is the feeling for words as living things, animated by the gestures of their production, enough to break open the gates of the prison? The dissolution of explication and the revocation of its sentences, far from putting a stop to study, reveal to us the poetry of words that carry on. As Rancière tells us, 'in the act of speaking, man doesn't transmit knowledge, he makes poetry … He communicates as an *artisan*: a person who handles words like tools.'[65] To communicate as a poet is to cherish words as the journeyman cherishes his equipment and materials. Every word is a jewel that sparkles like a pebble in the running water of a stream. We *feel* it in speaking, as it wells up in the cavity of the mouth and issues from the lively tongue and restless lips, or in writing as it is formed in the gestures and inflections of the hand. Hapticality, then, does not mean giving up on words or sinking beneath them. Nor can words themselves, spoken or written, be held to account for the stultifying effects of explication. Don't blame words for their incarceration; blame the court of explicators that has passed sentence on them.

What can the teacher teach?

To follow Rancière in overturning the myth of pedagogy is to acknowledge that what we do, as attentive and responsive beings, is neither to explain nor have things explained to us, but to make poetry together. But if emancipation lies thus in liberation from the prison-house of explication, then what happens to the explicators, to the schoolmasters or teachers of the old regime? What need have we of teachers at all? If they have nothing to explain, no knowledge to convey and no methods for doing so – if they are 'poor pedagogues' in Masschelein's terms, or weak educators in Biesta's – then what can teachers teach? The problem, for Rancière, is not with masters as such but with those who double up as explicators – that is, masters who attempt to combine their legitimate authority with the assumption of differential intelligence, as between their own enlightenment and the ignorance of their students.[66] Biesta agrees: indeed far from banishing teachers he insists, to the contrary, 'that teaching is a necessary component of all education'.[67] To give up on the idea that teachers have something to teach, Biesta declares, would be tantamount to giving up on the very idea of education.[68] He has good reason to be concerned, since he is writing against the background of overwhelming pressure, in the public and political mainstream, to reduce all education to learning, and in a narrow and impoverished sense of learning at that. I will have more to say on this reduction in the concluding section of this chapter. Let me focus for now on Biesta's key thesis, namely that *'to learn from someone is a radically different experience from the experience of being taught by someone'.*[69] What, then, is the difference between 'learning from' and 'being taught by'?

For Biesta, teaching is not a commandment but a gift. Like all gifts, however, it is not something in the teacher's power to give. A thing is not a gift a priori, but only becomes a gift when it is received as such. If it is refused, then it is not a gift at all but a discard. So too with teaching: it is only teaching when it is 'received' in the student's acknowledgement of having been taught. The teacher has no say in whether it will be received as such or not: he hopes it will be, but cannot determine the outcome. In this sense, as Biesta puts it, 'teaching is the giving of a gift the teacher doesn't possess'.[70] What is essential to education is that someone is present – let us call him the 'teacher' even though he is so only sporadically, in moments of acknowledgement – who is prepared to put what he has, indeed what he *is* (since in the process of study person and property are inseparable), 'on the table'. This was Dewey's answer to what he saw as the stupidity of simply leaving it up to learners to make of their education what they will. 'If the teacher is really a teacher', Dewey advised, 'he should know enough about his pupils, their needs, experiences, degrees of skill and knowledge, etc., to be able (not to dictate aims and plans) to share in a discussion regarding what is to be done'.[71] We may learn nothing *from* such a teacher, by way of substantive or informational content, but insofar as he demonstrates by example, keeps us – his pupils – on track, and verifies the results of our labours, we can claim to be taught by him. Here the teacher is exemplary in the conduct of study, a generous guide and companion for his students, and a tireless judge of their work.

This is not just a matter of scaffolding, or of providing the social support for learners to achieve what they could not do unaided, as classically advocated by the great pioneer of developmental psychology, Lev Vygotsky.[72] Influenced by

Vygotsky's theory, anthropologists such as Jean Lave and Barbara Rogoff have approached learning as a process of apprenticeship in which learners advance their skills and understanding through guided participation with more experienced partners in shared problem solving. In Lave's terms, apprenticeship is a matter of 'understanding in practice', by contrast to the idea of 'acquiring culture' central to orthodox models of learning as the intergenerational transmission of information.[73] Clearly, the apprenticeship model puts paid to the notion that individuals learn in isolation from one another, and in that regard is entirely consistent with Dewey's approach to education. Yet for Dewey there was more to it than that. Education depends on participation, to be sure, but not just on *any* participation. It has to be of a particular kind.

What is distinctive about educational participation, and marks it out from mere training – from preparation for entry into an established guild or profession – is that both teachers and learners, masters and students, share an interest in the process and stand to be transformed by it. This is the difference, as Biesta puts it, between 'educative and noneducative participation: participation in which only one party learns (by adapting to the other party), and participation that transforms the outlook of *all* who take part in it and that brings about a shared outlook'.[74] For Biesta, this is what distinguishes Dewey's 'education' from Lave's 'understanding in practice'. In our terms, it marks the difference between understanding and undercommoning, and likewise between solving problems and corresponding with them. Educative participation takes place in the milieu, in the midstream. Could we then follow Dewey's lead in thinking of teaching as a process of commoning and variation, of attention and response, in which master and students go along together in a spirit of patient experimentation, relating in the first place as persons with stories to tell, through endless cycles of demonstration, experimentation and verification, on and on to infinity? Then that infinity, as Rancière puts it, 'is no longer the master's secret; it is the student's journey'.[75] The book is finished, but the journey carries on indefinitely.

The learners' toolkit

Over the past year, a new feature has popped up on the desktop screen of every computer across the campus of the university where I work. It is called 'the learners' toolkit', and is indicated by a row of three thumbnail icons. Click on any icon, and a window will open up which provides much useful and well-intentioned advice for the perplexed student embarking on a university course. It offers, in its own words, '*tips, tools and techniques to make life at University easier*'. What caught my eye, however, were the icons themselves. The first depicts the outline of a head, but where the ears should be, it sprouts a pair of headphones. The second appears to show the rectangular screen of a smart-phone, with its rounded corners. In the third the head is back, but where the eyes should be, it wears shades. For my part, I possess neither headphones nor smart-phone, and use sunglasses only occasionally to protect my eyes from glare. But I do have my own toolkit, which I carry with me wherever I go. It also has three components: they are pencil, pocket notebook and spectacles. Suppose we put these toolkits side-by-side, the learners' and mine. The headphones: they conduct a feed into the brain, but the pencil? It ventures forth along a line that is always exploratory at the tip. What comes in through the phones is pre-composed; what goes out with the pencil is an improvisation. The smart-phone screen: at the touch of a finger it answers requests for information, in words and images, but the pages of my notebook? They offer fragments of memory, half-formed ideas caught on the fly, unfinished sentences full of crossings-out, word-lists, doodles, the detritus of a mind at work. The shades: they offer a protective shield to hide behind, but my spectacles? Of course I use them to read and write. They are instruments of attention, which compensate for my deteriorating eyesight. And they allow others to attend to me too, to see me eye-to-eye.

Comparing the two toolkits says much about the difference between the idea of learning, as it is increasingly understood today, and the idea of study I have advanced here. The iconic triptych of headphones, screen and shades paints to my mind a frightening picture of the idealised learner as currently conceived in a state-of-the-art, IT-obsessed educational environment. The learner of the toolkit appears to be an isolated individual, securely locked in and shielded from any sensory contact with the surroundings – from light by shades, from sound by phones (the head has no nose for scent, and being just a head, lacks hands to feel). This individual is completely immobile, but also placeless: indeed the blurb that accompanies the toolkit makes much of the fact that it is accessible on line, anywhere, anytime. But while blind and deaf to others, and to the world, our learner is fed with a continual stream of information, downloaded from remote sources into his head: visually, from the screen of his smart-phone; aurally through the phones that cover his ears. What kind of learning is this, which calls for no productive effort on the part of the learner, nor even for his presence, which replaces the teacher by a programme, which severs head from body, mind from world, and immunises the learner from the potentially corrupting effects of any disturbance from outside by means of a protective shield? In recent decades it has given rise to an entire industry, complete with its legions of providers, brands and watchwords. Biesta calls the industry 'learnification', a word whose sheer ugliness reflects his abhorrence of that to which it refers.[76]

Learnification, as Biesta shows, is what you get when education is subjected to the forces of the market, comprised in this case by individuals with needs and providers with the resources to satisfy them. With learnification the student is no longer a beginner who cannot yet know what his needs are but a customer who knows (or whose family knows) exactly what he needs, and is not afraid to demand immediate gratification. Newly placed in the driving seat, the student-customer is empowered to impose his own conditions on the transaction. The erstwhile pedagogue, once placed by his profession in a commanding position to dictate both the content of teaching and the manner of its delivery, finds himself recast as a service provider, a facilitator or even just a 'resource', whose role it is to provide the information that the individual learner has requested, in a way that makes it as easy for him as possible to assimilate and digest. In the brave new world of learnification, the *place* of learning – including its architecture and furniture – loses much of its significance. Classrooms that used to host practices of study are rebranded as resource centres, populated with banks of computers before which students, oblivious to their fellows, navigate the mazes of multiple choice. Chalkboards around which students and their teachers formerly gathered to write and draw, to comment and observe, have been stripped away to be replaced by slick white screens on which drawing and writing are forbidden; only the projection of images is permitted. In order that these images can be better seen, windows are covered by remote-controlled blinds to cut out the light. And the auditorium, once a place where students would assemble to *listen together*, and to share in the experience, becomes a theatre that serves only to achieve an economy of scale, whereby the same information can be simultaneously transmitted to hundreds of individual students.[77]

In an age of digital technology, however, simultaneous transmission can easily be achieved without having to assemble students in one place at all. If learning can be done anywhere, and if anyone can set up as a provider, why – some might ask – do we need schools or universities at all? Is technology making our traditional educational institutions redundant? The answer must be a resounding 'no'. For schools and universities are, before anything else, places of study. They are not, and have never been intended to be, 'learning environments' of the kind envisaged in the discourse of learnification. Study is the opposite, in every conceivable way, of the learning of the 'learners' toolkit'. It is about production rather than consumption, about making things public rather than their private appropriation. It gathers students and teachers together, around the table, rather than committing them to secure isolation. Of students and teachers alike, it demands that they make themselves present, in attention and response, rather than hiding behind the technology of transmission. Study carries on, in a process of perpetual beginning, rather than aiming towards the fulfilment of predefined ends. It is about generating interest in common, not about gratifying individual desires. It offers friendship, care and even love, but does not pretend to cater for individual well-being. Study is transformational; it is not training. Far from offering protection and security, or making things easy, study can be difficult and disturbing: it breaks down the defences of preconception and unsettles thought. Yet in so doing, it can set us free. With such disparity, it is no surprise that Biesta, for one, finds the new language of learning 'utterly unhelpful' in the double educational task of engagement and emancipation.[78] Indeed there is good reason to wonder whether learning in this sense has anything to do with education at all. I believe it does not.

Notes

1   Deleuze and Guattari (2004: 398–413).
2   Drawing on the writings of Giorgio Agamben, philosopher of education Tyson Lewis has advanced a rather similar argument: that to 'realise one's potential', in line with the majoritarian discourse of progressive pedagogy, is actually to eliminate it. To carry on we must remain with a 'pure potential' that is not given over to its actualisation. 'To think

pure potential freed from its subservience to actualization', Lewis writes, 'is not to follow the light' but 'to wander through darkness and shadow' (Lewis 2011: 594).

3 Harney and Moten (2013).

4 'Being lost emphasises in its absence the comfortable groundedness that is normally felt when one has found or is on the way. When lost, the ground feels less firm; the route less confidently "made" by each footstep for fear that it is leading one astray' (Vergunst 2008: 119).

5 Manning (2016).

6 Manning (2016: 138).

7 This is also the default position taken by mainstream cognitive psychology, in which the attribution of intentions to others, as a precondition for interaction, goes by the name of 'theory of mind'. Accordingly, autistics are characterised as individuals whose theory of mind is deficient, and who therefore fail in the attribution of mental states to others (see, for example, Baron-Cohen, Lombardo and Tager-Flusberg 1993). Needless to say, this kind of psychology itself suffers from an attention deficit that prevents it from even recognising, let alone comprehending, the emergent ecology of direct perception.

8 Manning (2016: 112).

9 Manning (2016: 14).

10 Manning (2016: 8).

11 Deleuze and Guattari (2004: 398).

12 Deleuze and Guattari (2004: 398–399).

13 Deleuze and Guattari (2004: 399).

14 Manning (2016: 13).

15 Ingold (2015: 139–140).

16 Manning (2016: 19).

17 Deleuze and Guattari (2004: 451).

18 Manning (2016: 20), emphases added.

19 Manning (2016: 118).

20 Ingold (2011: 211).

21 Ingold (2015: 23).

22 Manning (2016: 19).

23 Ingold (2015: 131).

24 Esposito (2012: 54).

25 Esposito (2012: 54).

26 Esposito (2012: 54).

27 Esposito (2012: 52).

28 Ingold (2015: 23).

29 Manning (2016: 134).

30 Deleuze and Guattari (2004: 4).

31 Deleuze and Guattari (2004: 13).

32 Manning (2016: 25), emphases added.

33 Manning (2016: 6).

34 Masschelein (2011: 530).

35 Masschelein (2011: 530).

36 Masschelein (2011: 530).

37 Manning (2016: 221).

38 Manning (2016: 10).

39 Manning (2016: 12).

40 Manning (2016: 39).

41 Manning (2016: 12).

42 Manning (2016: 12).

43 Manning (2016: 224).

44 Harney and Moten (2013: 110).

45 Harney and Moten (2013: 109).

46 Masschelein and Simons (2013: 40).
47 Masschelein and Simons (2013: 38).
48 Ingold (2015: 147–152).
49 Serres (1997: 5).
50 'Remarkably, the French language defines this word *milieu* as a point or an almost absent thread, as a plane or a variety with no thickness or dimension, and yet, all of a sudden, as the totality of the volume where we live: our environment. New reversal: from the half-place (*mi-lieu*), a small excluded locality, insignificant, ready to vanish, to the milieu (*milieu*), like a universe around us' (Serres 1997: 5).
51 Masschelein and Simons (2013: 36).
52 Pennac (2010: 50), cited in Masschelein and Simons (2013: 35).
53 Pennac (2010: 51).
54 Manning (2016: 12). As Tyson Lewis says of the time of study, it is neither 'not yet' nor 'no longer', but '*both* "no longer" *and* "not yet" simultaneously' (Lewis 2011: 592, original emphases). See also Ingold (2015: 146).
55 Masschelein and Simons (2013: 47).
56 Rancière (1991).
57 Rancière (1991: 7, original emphases).
58 Rancière (1991: 8, original emphases).
59 Polanyi (1966).
60 Manning (2016: 24).
61 Following the reintroduction of the concept of *habitus* into anthropology in the ethnological work of Marcel Mauss (1979), the primary responsibility for its current association with embodiment can be attributed to the sociological writings of Pierre Bourdieu (1977), in whose 'theory of practice' the principles of the *habitus* are said to be installed by way of 'structural exercises' that, as he puts it, never attain 'the level of discourse' (1977: 87–88). Psychologically, they remain underground, beyond the reach of consciousness. They cannot be articulated, or rendered explicit. Ineffable, incommunicable and therefore inimitable by any conscious effort, these principles are given body, made body, or literally *embodied*, in Bourdieu's words, 'by the hidden persuasion of an implicit pedagogy' (1977: 94).
62 Harney and Moten (2013: 98).
63 For a fuller discussion of this point, see Ingold (2013b: 109–111).
64 Polanyi (1958: 88).
65 Rancière (1991: 65, original emphasis).
66 Rancière (1991: 12–13).
67 Biesta (2013: 98).
68 Biesta (2013: 46).
69 Biesta (2013: 53, original emphases).
70 Biesta (2013: 139).
71 Dewey (1964: 154); from Dewey's essay 'Individuality and experience', first published in 1926.
72 Vygotsky (1978).
73 Lave (1990: 310). See also Lave (2011), Lave and Wenger (1991), Rogoff (1990, 2003).
74 Biesta (2013: 33, original emphasis).
75 Rancière (1991: 23).
76 Biesta (2013: 124).
77 Masschelein and Simons (2014).
78 Biesta (2013: 61).

4

ANTHROPOLOGY, ART AND THE UNIVERSITY

Anthropology *as* education

I am, by profession, an anthropologist. And for me, anthropology is a generous, open-ended, comparative, and yet critical inquiry into the conditions and potentials of human life in the one world we all inhabit. It is *generous* because it pays attention, and responds, to what other people do and say. In our inquiries we receive with good grace what is given rather than seek by subterfuge to extract what is not, and we are at pains to give back what we owe to others for our own intellectual, practical and moral formation. This happens, above all, in participant observation, and I shall return to this. Anthropology is *open-ended* because its aim is not to arrive at final solutions that would bring social life to a close but rather to reveal the paths along which it can keep on going. We are committed in this sense to sustainable living – to a form of sustainability that does not render the world sustainable for some through the exclusion of others, but rather has a place for everyone and everything. Anthropology is *comparative* because it acknowledges that no way of being is the only possible one, and that for every way we find, or resolve to take, alternative ways could be taken that would lead in different directions. No path is preordained as the only one that is 'natural'. Thus even as we follow a particular way, the question of 'why this way rather than that?' is always uppermost in our minds. And anthropology is *critical* because we cannot be content with things as they are. By general consent, the organisations of production, distribution, governance and knowledge that have dominated the modern era have brought the world to the brink of catastrophe. In finding ways to carry on, we need all the help we can get. But no-one – no indigenous group, no specialist science, no doctrine or philosophy – already holds the key to the future, if only we could find it. We have to make the future together, for ourselves. This however can only be achieved through dialogue. Anthropology exists to expand the scope of this dialogue: to make a conversation of human life itself.

Could not the same, however, be said of education? Does education not share the same defining characteristics: of generosity, open-endedness, comparison and criticality? Is its purpose not, likewise, to secure the continuity of life? That depends, of course, on what we mean by education, and there are certainly senses of the word, widely used today in policy and practice, which would satisfy none of these criteria. Neither a regime of command and obedience, as in the stereotypical Victorian schoolroom, nor one of commoditised service provision, as in the contemporary 'learning environment', is consistent with the principle of giving together (*com-munus*) that underwrites generous coexistence. An education that delivers an established curriculum towards predetermined outcomes can hardly be said to be open-ended. One that is single-track in its resolve to inculcate normative attributes, and that forges ahead with never a sideways glance, is scarcely comparative. And an education given over to critique, that trains its students in the arts of conjecture and refutation, or in the defence and attack of standpoints and perspectives, does little to instil the kind of critical thinking that could actually shift the ground of understanding. In previous chapters I have tried to show that there is another way of treating education. It is not new, having been adumbrated by Dewey a century ago. But it remains counter-hegemonic. My purpose in this final chapter is to demonstrate that the principles of education that Dewey proposed are indeed the principles of anthropology, and therefore that anthropology and education are parallel if not equivalent endeavours. Together, they have the potential to transform the world.

I shall proceed as follows. First, I will discuss what I take to be anthropology's most distinctive way of working, namely participant observation. Against the widely held idea of participant observation as an ethnographic method, I shall insist, to the contrary, that it enshrines an ontological commitment, an acknowledgement that we can know the world only because we are part of it, as science studies scholar Karen Barad puts it, in its 'differential becoming'.[1] Second, comparing what educationalists call 'school' with what anthropologists call 'the field', I will suggest that the practices of study are common to both, leading me to argue that the true purpose of anthropology is not ethnographic, as is often supposed, but educational. I will go on to show, third, how this way of thinking about anthropology brings it closely into alliance with art, but fourth, how at the same time it helps to close the gap between art and science that has been the source of so much rupture in the intellectual history of modernity. This leads me, fifth, to a series of broader concerns to do with the changing significance of the intellectual endeavour we call 'research', both in the arts and humanities and in the natural sciences, and to the relation between research and teaching, which I regard not as separate if complementary fields of activity but as inseparable aspects of the one task of education – a task that combines both care and curiosity. Sixth, I shall draw out the implications of this view of education for conceptions of the discipline and interdisciplinarity, arguing for a correspondence of lines of inquiry that is *anti*-disciplinary, insofar as it undercuts the territorialisation of knowledge implicit in conventional discourses of study. In the final two sections I return to the university as a place of higher education, the very existence of which is currently under attack as never before.

I will argue that the purposes of anthropology, of the university, and of education itself are intimately bound up with one another, and that their common future can only be secured through a fundamental revision of the principles of freedom and universality. Academic freedom, I argue, must be based on the principle of habit, not of volition. And the universe in which we study is founded not on essential similarity but on infinite difference.

Participant observation[2]

If ever there was a practice of exposure and of attention, of waiting on others, that leads us out into a world where we can share their company, that brings them into presence but at the same time unravels and un-destines, then it is surely the anthropological way of working we call participant observation. To observe means to watch what is going on around and about, and of course to listen and feel as well. To participate means to do so from within the current of activity in which you carry on a life alongside and together with the persons and things that capture your attention. Typically, the participant observer will spend an extended period, of many months or even years, joining in the lives of people in some place, or who are brought together around some activity, getting to know them and the things they have to deal with, on their own terms, as best she can, and learning from them in the process. In what anthropologists call 'the field' (of which more below), people are *there*: to be asked and answered to, to be observed but observant in their turn. Never in control of the situation, not knowing what any day will bring, the anthropological participant observer is vulnerable, largely at the mercy of unfolding events, and ever reliant on improvisation. Her questions are never exhausted by their answers but always give way to further questioning, none of which comes any closer to a solution but which nevertheless opens up to an ongoing process of life. There is nothing peculiar about this. Indeed, anthropological participant observation differs only in degree of intensity from what all people do all of the time: it is not just an anthropological way of working but a condensed expression of the way we all work. For the anthropologist's 'field', as I shall show, is none other than an undercommons, and the undercommons, as we discovered in Chapter 3, is always there, even if we are loath to admit it.

It is sometimes supposed that participation and observation are in contradiction. How can one simultaneously watch what is going on and join in? Recall the image, from Serres, of the two rivers. There's the river we see flowing by as we stand on the banks. And there's the river experienced by the swimmer breasting the current of the midstream. Is participant observation not tantamount to asking us to inhabit both rivers at the same time? 'One can observe and participate', writes anthropologist Michael Jackson, 'successively but not simultaneously'.[3] For, as he goes on to explain, observation and participation yield different kinds of data, respectively objective and subjective. How can the engagement of participation possibly be combined with the detachment of observation? These questions, however, are couched in the metaphysical register, with its a priori appeal to transcendent humanity. This register, deeply rooted in the protocols of normal science, drives a wedge between our ways of knowing *about* the world and our ways of being *in* it. As human beings, it seems, we can aspire to knowledge of the world only by way of an emancipation that takes us from it and leaves us strangers to ourselves. It is as though we can no longer exist in the world we seek to know.[4] The alleged contradiction between participation and observation is no more than a corollary of this excision of being from knowing, ontology from epistemology. If ever we are to understand, according to science, we must set aside the subjective experience that comes from swimming in the midstream and regain our foothold on the banks, whence we can look back on it objectively, from the safety and security of our respective positions. In this very move, what we have undergone *with* people is converted into a test that we have willingly put ourselves through in order to make a study *of* them. It is, so to speak, to put in brackets the attentional 'doing undergoing' of common life, only to reframe it as an undergoing within the intentional doing of fieldwork. And this is what happens when we say that what we were actually doing, with participant observation, is *ethnography*.

With ethnography, our teachers are recast as objects of study. This is like turning a telescope to look through the wrong end. Instead of calling on the experience of those among whom we have lived to enlarge our vision of the world, we take our sights from the Olympian heights of 'theory' to scrutinise the thinking of our erstwhile companions, which now figures as 'data' for analysis. The source of the problem, I believe, lies in that little word *of*. For whenever we invoke the anthropology *of* this or that, it is as though we run rings around the thing in question, turning the places or the paths from which we observe into circumscribed topics of inquiry. '*Of*-ness', as noted in Chapter 2, converts the other with which one corresponds into its object, observation into objectification. Observation, as Jackson tells us in this vein, yields 'objective data'.[5] But to observe *with* or *from* is not to objectify; it is to *attend* to persons and things, to learn from them, and to follow in precept and practice. This is how the apprentice observes in the practice of a skill, how the devotee observes in the routines of worship, how the anthropologist observes in the tasks of everyday life in the field. Whereas *of*-ness is intentional, *with*-ness is attentional. And what it sets up is a participatory coupling, in perception and action, of observer and observed. This is to choose existence over essence, to reunite knowing with being, and to restore observation to participation in a life lived in the company of others. Indeed in the register of existence, of common life, there can be no observation without participation. Thus participant observation is absolutely *not* an under-cover technique for gathering intelligence on people, on the pretext of learning from them. It is rather a fulfilment, in both letter and deed, of what we owe to the world for our development and formation. That is what I mean by ontological commitment.

To practise participant observation, however, is also to undergo an education. Indeed I believe there are grounds for substituting the word 'education' for 'ethnography' as the most fundamental purpose of anthropology. I do not mean by this to give a boost to that minority if unjustly neglected subfield known as the anthropology of education. I want to insist, rather, on anthropology as a *practice* of education. It is a practice dedicated to what anthropologist Kenelm Burridge has called *metanoia*: 'an ongoing series of transformations each one of which alters the predicates of being'.[6] That, of course, is just another way of reformulating Dewey's 'principle of habit', according to which 'every experience enacted and undergone modifies the one who acts and undergoes'.[7] Though Burridge argues that metanoia is the goal of ethnography, to my mind it much more appropriately describes the goal of education. Jackson, in his own work, offers a fine example. Much of Jackson's anthropological research was carried out among Kuranko people in the West African country of Sierra Leone. This country, he acknowledges, 'transformed me, shaping the person I now am and the anthropology I do'. Exactly so: but that is why, to my mind, the anthropology he does is a practice of education and *not* of ethnography. 'I have never thought of my research among the Kuranko as elucidating a unique lifeworld or foreign worldview', Jackson admits. 'Rather, this was the laboratory in which I happened to explore the *human* condition'.[8] Exploring the conditions and possibilities of being human: that's what anthropology *is*. And that, too, is what Jackson is doing with his Kuranko hosts. Precisely because his aim is to conduct such an exploration, and *not* to elucidate specific features of the Kuranko lifeworld, it is not ethnography. Why then, despite all this, does he continue to portray himself as an ethnographer?

Elsewhere, however, Jackson comes close to defining his anthropological project in educational terms: it is, he says, about 'opening up new possibilities for thinking about experience' – a process which, following the philosopher Richard Rorty, he calls *edification*.[9] For Rorty, to edify is to keep the conversation going and, by the same token, to resist all claims to final, objective solutions. It is to open a space, he writes, 'for the sense of wonder which poets can sometimes cause – wonder that there is something new under the sun, something which is *not* an accurate representation of what was already there, something which (at least for the moment) cannot be explained and can barely be described'.[10] Does this sense of wonder, which Rorty attributes to the poet, not also lie at the root of anthropological sensibility? Recall Rancière's observation, from the last chapter, that there is poetry in human communication, in the sharing of feeling, in the hapticality of the undercommons. The poet, after all, writes not *up* but *with*. William Wordsworth was not, in his poetry, writing up his walks in the English Lake District: rather his writing, like his wandering, was a correspondence with the land in which we too can join as we embark with him in our reading. Cannot anthropologists also be poets? Indeed some are, notably including Jackson, but here I don't mean that we should write poetry on the side, as if to add a second string to our bow, but that we might find, in our writing, a way of opening up to the world, as we do in dreams, where imagination and reality are one. Such writing might have the capacity not just to inform but to inspire.

Like poetry, anthropology both wonders and wanders. The wondering lies in attention, the wandering in following. The novice-anthropologist is called upon both to attend to what others are doing or saying and to what is going on around and about, and to follow along where others go and to do their bidding, whatever this might entail and wherever it might take you. This exposure can be unnerving, and entails considerable existential risk. It is like pushing the boat out into an as yet unformed world – a world in which things are not ready made but always incipient, on the cusp of continual emergence. Commanded, as Masschelein puts it, not by the given but by what is *on the way* to being given, one has to be prepared to wait.[11] Waiting upon things is precisely what it means to attend to them. And as every anthropologist knows, more of the time of participant observation is spent in waiting for people to turn up and for things to happen than is ever spent in full-on activity.

The school and the field

To practice participant observation, then, is to join in correspondence with those among whom we study. Herein, I think, lies the educational purpose, dynamic and potential of anthropology. As such, it is the very opposite of ethnography. For the aim of ethnography, to return to Jackson's distinction, is precisely to 'elucidate a life-world' rather than to 'explore the human condition'.[12] It is to render an account – in writing, film or other graphic media – of life as it is actually lived, thought and experienced, by a people, somewhere, sometime. Good ethnography is contextually nuanced, richly detailed, and above all faithful to what it depicts. These are all admirable qualities. But they are not the qualities to which anthropology aspires. This aspiration, in the field as in the school, is to study *with* people; not to make studies *of* them. We do not, after all, seek to study with great scholars in order that we can spend the rest of our lives describing, representing and analysing their philosophies or worldviews. The purpose of academic study is not to put everything our professors say in context, by a detailed accounting of their words or a nuanced analysis of their ideas. It does not commit us to fidelity in rendering the master's voice. To receive the gift of teaching is to enter imaginatively into the world our teachers open for us, and to join with them in its exploration; it is not to close that world down. But if that is so, and if – as I have intimated – to practise anthropology is to undergo an education, as much beyond as within the academy, then what goes for our participation with academic correspondents must hold, equally, for our 'non-academic' correspondents as well. Why should it be any different? In the field as in the school, we study so that we can grow ourselves, in knowledge, wisdom and judgement, and in order to be better prepared for the tasks that lie ahead in building a common world. Knowledge is knowledge, wherever it is grown, and if our purpose in developing it within the academy is educational rather than ethnographic, then so it should be beyond the academy as well.

Indeed there are many similarities between the school and the field, regarded as places of study, and much that I have said in the last chapter about what it means to study could apply equally to the conduct of anthropological fieldwork. Study in the field is communal rather than solitary, it follows real problems but not to find solutions, it is speculative but not predictive, critical but not wedded to critique.

Like the school, in the weak sense of *scholè*, the field is an undercommons, alive with minor gestures. Fieldwork is not the application of method in order to obtain results, but a practice of patient experimentation which converts every answer into a question. When Moten says of study in the undercommons, that 'it's talking and walking around with other people', or when Harney describes it as 'where you allow yourself to be possessed by others as they do something', they could be referring to study in the field just as well as in school.[13] It follows however that the anthropologist's 'field' is not quite the same as 'everyday life' for her hosts, as though the exposure were entirely on the side of the former, leaving the latter to carry on with business as usual. The parallel with school suggests, to the contrary, that for the hosts, too, the field is a place out of quotidian time, where normal expectations are suspended or held in abeyance, where things are defamiliarised and disappropriated. It is a milieu, a middle-place, wherein the world opens up not only for the anthropologist but for her hosts as well. This is the very opening that allows undercommoning (rather than understanding) to proceed.

Not all participation, then, is anthropological, and we should be equally sceptical of those who offer participation as a panacea for 'user-centred' research, as of the agents of learnification who market participation as the magic ingredient of 'student-centred' education. Just as there is a difference, as Biesta insists, between participation that is educative and participation that is not,[14] so we can say of participant observation, too, that it is only anthropological when it transforms the outlook of *all* participants. Simply adapting – learning to 'fit in' with what others do or say as a matter of course – may suffice for the collection of ethnographic data, but it harbours no transformative potential. Recall that this potential – the excess of commoning and variation over the mere conveyance of information – was for Dewey precisely what sets education apart from training. For us likewise, it separates anthropology from ethnography. There is a temporal dimension, too, to this separation. Anthropology, as Manning would say, is 'in the event'.[15] As a way of knowing from the inside, it proceeds through interstitial differentiation, inflected by the modifications that accompany every enactment of experience. The time it takes is time spent going along together in what Manning calls 'mobile coexistence'[16] – that is, in correspondence. Ethnography, on the other hand, offers a retrospective account: an abduction from events that have already occurred to the intentions that motivated them and the contexts in which they were embedded, and a retracing of the causal relations that gave rise to them. Anthropology's correspondence is ethnography's backgridding.

The participant observer who would fain position herself in the field as an ethnographer is consequently liable to be caught facing in two ways at once. In what is often called the 'ethnographic encounter' she ostensibly joins with others, bringing them into her presence as she into theirs, only to turn her back on them as if they were not there. For to mark the encounter as ethnographic is to consign the incipient – the about-to-happen in unfolding relationships – to the temporal past of the already over. Anthropologist Johannes Fabian refers to this two-faced stance as one of 'schizochrony'.[17] This, rather than any contradiction between participation and observation, is the real dilemma that comes from the attempted conflation of anthropology and ethnography. It is the reason why so much emphasis is placed on the establishment of 'rapport', in the field, between the ethnographer and her hosts. For in combining the connotations of rapprochement and rapportage, 'rapport' is similarly schizochronic. It means overtly attending to others with the concealed intention of reporting on them.[18] As everyone accepts, rapport takes time to build, but this is time not for correspondence but for a kind of cognitive excavation – an elicitation of concepts and categories that could eventually uncover a common ground of understanding. Now correspondence, too, takes time, but this is time devoted to an imaginative stretch of attention by which both parties – anthropologist and hosts – reach an accord that goes *beyond* existing understandings. Nor is there any end to this. Ethnography imposes its own finalities on trajectories of study, ultimately converting them into data-gathering exercises destined to yield 'results', usually in the form of research papers or monographs. But the point about anthropology, as Dewey said of education, is not that it should end in final outcomes but that it should open up to experiences that themselves open to further experience, making possible a never-ending and always beginning process of growth and discovery. Final outcomes spell the death of anthropology, as indeed they do of education.

Are artists the real anthropologists?

I began this chapter by declaring my professional identity as an anthropologist. Yet for several years now, something has been pulling on my disciplinary moorings. For I have a nagging sense that the people really doing anthropology, these days, are artists. Not all artists, to be sure. 'Art' covers such a broad spectrum, and embraces such an eccentric assortment of practices, that attempts to pin it down to a single definition are bound to founder on the rocks of exception. The interminable discourses generated in these attempts, while they have advanced many academic careers, lead nowhere save back into their own impenetrable undergrowth. Of a work or a performance, 'is it art?' is about the least interesting question to ask. We can however ask what makes art anthropological. Art that is anthropological, in my terms, is characterised – as is anthropology – by generosity, open-endedness, comparison and criticality. It is inquisitive rather than interrogative, offering a line of questioning rather than demanding answers; it is attentional, rather than fronted by prior intentions, modestly experimental rather than brazenly transgressive, critical but not given over to critique. Joining with the forces that give birth to ideas and things, rather than seeking to express what is already there, art that is anthropological conceives without being conceptual. Such art rekindles care and longing, allowing knowledge to grow from the inside of being in the correspondences of life.

This is why such practices as walking, drawing, calligraphy, instrumental music, dance, ways of making and working with materials – ways that tend to get bracketed at the 'craft' end of the spectrum – are exemplary for me. Artists engaging in these practices come closest, in my view, to doing real anthropology, even if they do not self-consciously present their work as such. But when it comes to anthropologists themselves, for the most part they are not doing real anthropology in this sense. They have instead settled for ethnography. If they distinguish anthropology from ethnography at all – and the majority do not – then their anthropology usually comes in afterwards, following an initial phase of 'writing up' the findings from ethnographic fieldwork, at the point when they turn from analysing empirical data to theoretical generalisation. At this point what had once been a life lived with others becomes a 'case' for comparison. Life is open-ended, but the case is closed, property of the ethnographer. It is this three-stage model – collect the data, pack it up, then compare – leading from initial encounter to final outcome, that renders ethnography as a *method*, a technique of collection, and as a means to ends that are ultimately anthropological. And it is largely as a method that ethnography has been appropriated by certain tendencies in contemporary art which self-consciously present themselves as 'anthropological'.

Indeed the majority of explicit attempts to marry anthropology and art have singled out ethnography as the cement that holds them together. These attempts, however, have not been wholly successful. For a start, artists rarely make good ethnographers. Observational detail and descriptive fidelity are not prized by the artists of today as they were in the past. The Dutch masters of the seventeenth century, who practised what has aptly been called 'the art of describing', arguably set a precedent for the European and American ethnographers of the twentieth: what the former achieved through layering oils on canvas the latter achieved through weaving words into texts. Indeed the very notion of 'thick description' echoes the opacity of oil-paint.[19] But such description holds little appeal to an art of the contemporary that is nothing if not speculative. Moreover art's turn to ethnography brings in train two preoccupations that do much to undermine its anthropological promise. Already adumbrated over two decades ago, in an influential paper aptly entitled 'The artist as ethnographer?' by critic and historian Hal Foster, the first lies in an obsession with *alterity*; the second in the insistence on placing every matter of concern in its social, cultural and historical *context*.[20]

Anthropologists like to impress their friends with stories of their encounter with 'radical alterity'. For some it is almost a badge of honour that confers the right to speak of otherness – of its political force or transgressive potential – with an authority denied to their less seasoned or adventurous cousins. It is a badge that many artists, consumed by what Foster calls 'ethnographer envy', would dearly love to wear.[21] This does beg the question, however, of how 'other' the people have to be in order that their alterity should count as radical. Simply to ask the question reveals the familiar calculus of sameness and difference that sorts people into cultures and subcultures depending on how much or how little they have primordially in common. Everyone is different but some, it seems, are more different than others, and some are even *radically* different. There is no need to rehearse our critique of the logic of cultural transmission on which this calculus rests. Suffice it to say that the anthropological field of participant observation is one in which difference draws people together in commoning rather than dividing them in the contraposition of their respective identities. It is a field not of othering but *togethering*.

Indeed participant observation can only begin from the acknowledgement that others are others, not because they are set apart on opposite sides of a frontier between cultural worlds, ours and theirs, but because they are fellow travellers with us in the *same* world. Herein, as we have seen, lies its ontological commitment. It is a commitment to the habitation not of multiple worlds of being, but of one becoming world of nevertheless infinite multiplicity. Difference, in this 'worlding' world, is interstitial: it is generated from the inside, not in the collage-like juxtaposition of worlds that are radically outside one another. The inherent schizochrony of the ethnographic stance, however, by placing alterity ahead of difference, turns its back on others and converts them into surrogates for an idealised projection of the anthropological or artistic self. It leads to the coding of difference as manifest identity and of otherness as outsideness. And as Foster points out, this can be just a prelude for a politics of marginality from which others are effectively excluded, rather than one of immanence in which all can join on an equal footing.[22]

This marginalisation of others is only compounded by the insistence on placing them in context. It is, as we saw in Chapter 2, to neutralise the force of their presence, to quell their discord, and make them safe. Thus understood and accounted for, disarmed and laid to rest, we are no longer troubled to attend to them or to what they have to say. Whether of persons or things, their contextualisation does not bring them *forth* to be themselves, but refers them *back*, to what anthropologist Alfred Gell has called the 'complex intentionalities' that are supposed to have supplied their motivation.[23] Indeed it is by their embodiment or as precipitates of such intentionalities that objects or performances qualify, for Gell, as artworks. To apprehend the work as art, he tells us, we have to be able to read these intentionalities, for the purposes of which 'an interpretative context has to be developed and disseminated'.[24] In this endeavour, the artist joins with the critic and the historian of art: they are all in it together, complicit in marking things – matters of concern – with the imprimatur of their special creativity or expertise, and appointing themselves to the task of lifting the veil on their significance to a public whose sense of intellectual inferiority, in comparison to the experts, is thereby reproduced. Galleries, then, become places not for the presentation of work but for its explication, from which visitors emerge knowing everything there is to be known about how and why the work was produced, by whom and when, in what cultural context and as part of what historical movement, but without ever having experienced the work, *as art*, at all. It might as well not be there.

Gell's proposal for the alliance of art with anthropology does nothing to challenge this hierarchy of interpretative prowess. On the contrary, it is only reinforced. The proposal is that anthropologists join with the artists, critics and historians, allowing a much wider range of things – gathered from peoples around the world – to be admitted to the special reserve of artworks, and offering their ethnographic expertise to supply the necessary contexts of interpretation. Behind all the posturing, this move is as reactionary as it is complacent. For what history and criticism does for art is precisely what ethnography does for anthropology. It kills it off. I have argued, to the contrary, that the promise of anthropology is to bring others to life, to draw them into the field of our attention so that we, in turn, can correspond with them. A work of art can be anthropological, insofar as it delivers on this promise: if it serves to bring things forth into the fullness of presence, to put them 'on the table', to free them from the determinations of aims and objectives. Art that is anthropological allows things to *be themselves*.

In his essay *Point and Line to Plane*, the pioneer of modern abstract painting Wassily Kandinsky had just this to say about the elements of a work of art. Any element, he wrote, can be experienced either outwardly or inwardly. Outwardly, it is simply doing its job within the conventions of a notational system, as the full stop, for example, marks the end of a sentence. So long as we remain at this mundane level, we are indifferent to the stop as a figure in its own right. Sunk into its context of use, we scarcely even notice it. But as soon as we revoke the stop from its sentence and enlarge its mass, it is revealed as a point whose forces are about to burst from the depths of its being and radiate their energy. 'In short', writes Kandinsky, 'the dead point becomes a living thing'.[25] To apprehend the point inwardly is to feel its explosive potential. This inherent hapticality is what makes Kandinsky's art – shaped as it was by his formative experiences of the animism and shamanic practices of Finno-Ugric and Siberian peoples – so intuitively anthropological.[26]

The softening of science

Let me return to the three-stage model by which anthropology has classically been distinguished from ethnography.[27] Far from aligning anthropology with art, the original ambition that lay behind the model – as set out by the founding fathers of social anthropology, most notably A. R. Radcliffe-Brown – was to establish the discipline as a *science*, indeed nothing less than a 'natural science of society'.[28] According to Radcliffe-Brown and his followers, ethnography is 'idiographic', in that it is dedicated to the collection of empirical particulars, while anthropology is 'nomothetic', dedicated to comparative generalisation and the search for law-like regularities in the conduct of human relations.[29] Between the first stage of collection and the final stage of comparison, the second stage of analysis processes the materials from the first into cases for comparison in the third. In application, the effect of this model has been to align the distinction between ethnography and anthropology to that between empirical and theoretical inquiry. Indeed for many, the word 'anthropology' still has a theoretical ring about it: unlike hands-on fieldwork, it is often felt to be something in which senior scholars can indulge, once they have retreated to the comfort of their armchairs. I have argued, to the contrary, that anthropology is anything but comfortable, and that it comes not last but first. It is what we do in the course of participant observation in the field, precisely because participant observation is *not* a technique of data collection – not, at least, in the sense by which data are defined under the regime of normal science. It is rather a practice of education, a course of study, undertaken in the field rather than the school. Can my kind of anthropology, then, only ever be an art of inquiry? Must it necessarily fail as science?

The answer depends on what we mean by data. Literally, of course, a datum is that which is given. In his aptly titled book, *Art, Anthropology and the Gift*, Roger Sansi observes that the theme of giving and receiving has always been central to anthropology, as indeed to art, not only because of its ubiquity in the conduct of human affairs, but also because it is inherent in fieldwork practice itself.[30] Herein lies the essential generosity of the discipline to which I have already referred. This generosity, however, does not sit readily with the protocols of normal science which require, in the name of objectivity, that we sever all personal relations with the things we study, and remain unmoved and unperturbed by their condition. We owe them nothing, according to these protocols, and they offer us nothing in return. Indeed, for the scientist even to admit to a relationship of give and take with the things in the world with which he deals would be enough to disqualify the inquiry and any insights arising from it. For what science counts as data have not been bestowed as any kind of gift or offering. In their collection, scientists do not so much receive what is given as take what is not, by resort to stratagems of deceit and trickery built into the design of what they call 'experiments'.

The scientific experiment, however, is a test, wilfully inflicted, an undergoing in doing; it is not an experience enacted and undergone as in 'doing undergoing'. That is to say, it is framed by the principle of volition, not of habit. As we have seen, even anthropologists are inclined – in their retrospective accounting of fieldwork as ethnography – to describe it as a prolonged experiment of this kind, which they have put themselves through in order to gather intelligence from 'informants' while pretending to learn from them. Such is the price of anthropology's attempt to pass itself off as a science of society. In this attempt, however, anthropology is bound to come across as methodologically compromised, its claims to objectivity fatally undermined by the fieldworker's unavoidable entanglements with other lives. For what is the role of methodology, if not to confer immunity to any infection stemming from immediate contact with others? Casting ways of working within a procedural logic that is indifferent to human experience and sensibility, methodology treats the presence of the observer in the field of inquiry not as an essential prerequisite for learning from what the world has to offer, but as a source of bias to be reduced at all cost. Any science that fails in this regard is considered – usually unfavourably – to be 'soft', and anthropology by that measure is positively squishy!

Hard science, when it comes up against other things in the world, has an impact. It can hit them, or even break them. Every hit is a datum; if you accumulate enough data, you may achieve a breakthrough. The surface of the world has yielded under the impact of your incessant blows, and having done so, releases some of its secrets. Soft science, by contrast, bends and deforms when it encounters other things, taking into itself some of their characteristics while they, in turn, bend to its pressure in accordance with their own inclinations and dispositions. It responds to things as they to it. To enter thus into a relation of correspondence with persons or things is the very opposite of the application of robust methodology. Far from forging an impregnable shield that would protect the investigator from having to share in the suffering of those subjected to his hard-ball tactics, correspondence amounts to a way of working, akin to a craft, which opens up the world to our perception, to what is going on there, so that we in turn can answer to it. It is driven neither by violence nor by deception but by hope: the hope that by paying attention to the beings and things with which we deal, they in turn will attend to us, and respond to our overtures.

In participant observation, as we have seen, anthropologists become correspondents. They take into themselves something of their hosts' ways of moving, feeling and thinking, their practical skills and modes of attention. Correspondence is a labour of love, of giving back what we owe to the human and non-human beings with which and with whom we share our world, for our own existence. If anthropology, then, is a science, it is a *science of correspondence*. Two centuries ago, Johann Wolfgang von Goethe proposed just such a science: one that demanded of practitioners that they should spend time with the objects of their attention, observe closely and with all their senses, draw what they observed, and endeavour to reach a level of mutual involvement, in perception and action, such that observer and observed become all but indistinguishable.[31] It is from this crucible of mutual involvement, Goethe argued, that all knowledge grows. The parallels with the much more recent injunctions of participant observation in anthropology are striking: what we are exhorted to do with the people with whom we work – to spend time with them, join in their activities of daily life, observe closely and record – Goethe was already urging scientists to do with animals and plants, back in the eighteenth century. Yet contemporary attitudes to what is nowadays called 'Goethean science', in the technoscientific mainstream, are telling. It is commonly regarded with a degree of indifference bordering on contempt; its practitioners are ridiculed and its submissions for publication systematically rejected. Methodology, not correspondence, is the order of the day.

It has not always been thus. Earlier periods in the history of science saw none of the polarisation that is in such stark evidence today. There seems little doubt that recent decades have seen a pronounced 'hardening' of science which can readily be linked, as we shall see below, to its marketisation as the engine of a global knowledge economy. For the commoditisation of knowledge requires that the fruits of scientific endeavour be broken off from the currents of life, from their ebbs and flows, and from their mutual entailments. This breach is effected by methodology: thus the harder the science, the more robust the methodology. The effect of relentless competition for 'innovation' and 'excellence' has been to power a kind of methodological arms race that draws scientists ever further from the phenomena they profess to study, and increasingly into virtual worlds of their own making. Yet however tenuous the connection with the real, it cannot be entirely broken. For in the final resort, there can be no science without observation, and no observation without the observer's attention being closely attuned to those aspects of the world with which it is joined. To highlight these observational commitments – to attend to the practices of science rather than its protocols – means recovering those very experiential and performative engagements which methodology goes to such lengths to cover up. For in practice, scientists too are inhabitants of the undercommons, immersed in hapticality, ever attentive and responsive to the rust-lings and whisperings of their surroundings. The chemist Friedrich August Kekulé, in a lecture recalling his discovery of the structure of the benzene molecule, offered this advice to every young scientist: 'note every footprint, every bent twig, every fallen leaf'. Then, he said, you will see where next to place your feet. For Kekulé, science was a sort of wayfaring, or as he called it, 'pathfinding'.[32]

Corresponding with things in the processes of their formation, rather than merely being informed by what has already precipitated out, the pathfinder not only collects but *accepts* what the world has to offer. It is in this more humble profession, I believe, rather than in arrogating to itself the exclusive authority to represent a given reality, that scientific inquiry can converge with artistic sensibility as a way of knowing-in-being.[33] Scientists' hands and minds, like those of artists or craftspeople, absorb into their ways of working a perceptual acuity attuned to the materials that have captured their attention, and as these materials vary, so does the experience that comes from working with them. Surely in practice, scientists are differentiated – as much as are artists and anthropologists, and indeed people everywhere – by the specificities of their experience and the skills arising from them, not by the territorial demarcation of fields of study. Science, when it becomes art, is both personal and charged with feeling; its wisdom is born of imagination and experience, and its manifold voices belong to each and every one who prac-tices it, not to some transcendent authority for which they serve indifferently as spokespersons. And where scientific pathfinding joins with the art of inquiry, as in the practice of anthropology, to grow into knowledge of the world is at the same time to grow into the knowledge of one's own self.

Search, and search again[34]

I have shown that science has the potential to be an art of inquiry, and that art, by the same token, can be a practice of science. Where science and art converge is in the *search for truth*. By truth I do not mean fact rather than fantasy, but the unison of experience and imagination in a world to which we are alive and that is alive to us. It is a great mistake to confuse the pursuit of truth with the pursuit of objectivity. For if the latter prescribes that we cut all ties with the world, the former demands our full and unqualified participation. It demands acknowledgement of what we owe to the world for our own existence and formation, as living beings within it, as well as of what the world owes to us. Research, I contend, is a way of sustaining this relation of mutual indebtedness. As such, it entails both curiosity and care. We are curious about the well-being of people we know and love, and never miss an opportunity to ask them how they are doing. That is because we care about them. Should it not be the same for the world around us? We are curious *because* we care. We care about the earth and all its inhabitants, human and non-human. We care about the past, because it helps us to better know ourselves and where we have come from. And we care about the future because when we are gone we want to leave behind a world that is habitable for the generations that come after us. In short, curiosity and care are two sides of the same coin. That coin is truth. Research, then, is *the pursuit of truth through the practices of curiosity and care*.

Admittedly, truth can mean different things, depending on a scholar's doctrine or philosophy. What is truth for a physicist may not be what it is for a theologian, an anthropologist or a musician. Nevertheless the *search* for truth is common to all. It is about trying to get things right: empirically, intellectually, ethically, or aesthetically. To embark on such a search is not like entering a maze or setting out on a treasure-hunt, where the object of desire is already there, ready and waiting, if only one could find it. Truth is an aspiration: it is what we reach for, long for, but ever evades our grasp. The closer we get to it, the more it recedes beyond the horizon of conceptualisation. The search for truth, then, will not deliver final answers, nor is that its purpose. It is rather to suspend all prejudice or presupposition, to turn all certainty into questioning. You think you already know the answer? Assuredly you do not. Search again, and again, and again! That – to search again – is what the word 'research' literally *means*. With no prospect of ultimate delivery into light, research is unremittingly in the minor key, ever in the shadow of illumination. Intense and concentrated research, as educational philosopher Tyson Lewis says, has an infernal quality: 'without clear direction, without a clear methodology, without an end in sight, we stumble along on a quest for new clues'.[35] Scholars are anxious souls! Yet they are also hopeful, for as an itinerant task of patient experimentation, research converts every closure into an opening, every apparent end-point into a new beginning. It is the guarantor that life can carry on, of its continuity. And for this reason, research is a primary responsibility of the living.

Nevertheless as Dewey recognised, every generation must eventually give way to the next, and as lives overlap, continuity depends upon each playing its part in establishing the conditions of development for its successors. That is why there cannot be research without teaching. All study, as Rancière for one has insisted, is research, and all research necessarily goes on under the ever-vigilant eye of a master or teacher. 'The master', says Rancière, 'is he who keeps the researcher on his route, the one that he alone is following and keeps following'.[36] Both teaching and research, then, are practices of education, and both are inextricably linked in just the same way that for Dewey, older and younger generations contribute to each other's formation. Teaching is the gift that the older generation offers to the younger – the gift it does not possess – in deferred return for the gift it received from *its* seniors. That is how life and knowledge are carried on. And it is why research, as the production of new knowledge, cannot be *opposed* to teaching as its dissemination. This opposition belongs to the language of explication. In this language the research comes first, and only its finished products, its results, are handed down by the teacher. The education of students is here construed as an inessential add-on to research, often perceived by researchers themselves as an unwelcome chore and a distraction from their primary concerns. 'My teaching', complains the frustrated scholar, 'leaves me with no time for research!' Recognising that research is something that teachers and students do together makes nonsense of such complaints. For research does not precede teaching as production to dissemination. It wells up under the eyes of teaching only to become those eyes, allowing a new generation to begin under their watch. When we say – as we like to do, and with good cause – that our teaching is 'research-led', this does not mean that our students receive their knowledge at first rather than second hand. It means, rather, that teacher and students are together immersed, as companions and fellow travellers, in a milieu – a 'second river', as Serres would put it – dedicated to the search for truth.

Now in our present global predicament, to idealise research as the pursuit of truth, grounded in curiosity and care, is likely to sound incorrigibly starry-eyed, even nostalgic. 'Get real!' I hear you say. 'If you want to make a better world for future generations, then by all means try, but to make any progress you will need to secure funding, show results, and make sure they win over those of your competitors.' In short, to do research and succeed in it you have to play a game, the rules and rewards of which are determined by governments and corporations already locked into the inexorable logic of globalisation. This logic, however, has corrupted the meaning of 'research' beyond recognition. It no longer has much to do with the kind of critical study that we used to call 'scholarship'. Indeed scholarship has been virtually relegated to the dustbin of academic work that is practically useless, a drain on the public purse, and destined for obscurity. Real research, we are told, is about the production of knowledge, the value of which is to be measured by its novelty rather than by any appeal to truth. Most funded research nowadays involves the extraction of large quantities of 'data', and their processing by means of programmes into 'outputs' which – in their potential application – could have an 'impact'. In the neoliberal economy of knowledge, change and innovation are of the order of the day, since as the resources of the planet run dry and in an ever more intense competition for dwindling returns, only what is new sells. 'Excellent research', in the macabre language of corporate capitalism, 'drives innovation'.

True, much of the research being carried on in what is increasingly known as 'academia' is not geared towards immediate application. It is said to be curiosity-driven, or 'blue sky'. Scientists have been vociferous in defending their right to undertake blue-sky research, albeit at considerable public expense, pointing time and again to a string of discoveries that, only long after they were made, turned out to be of such practical benefit that we now depend on them for our everyday lives. But in the land of academia, curiosity has been divorced from care, freedom from responsibility. As a net importer of services, academia's income is derived from its exports of knowledge, but it is left to those who buy the knowledge to determine how it should be applied, whether to build bombs, cure disease, or rig markets. Why should scientists care? This attitude, widespread among practitioners of the so-called STEM subjects (science, technology, engineering and mathematics), reveals the lofty appeal to blue skies to be little more than a smokescreen for science's abject surrender to the market model of knowledge production. It amounts to a self-serving defence of special interests increasingly concentrated in the hands of a global scientific elite which, in collusion with the corporations it serves, treats the rest of the world – including the vast majority of its increasingly impoverished and apparently disposable human population – as little more than a standing reserve for the supply of data to feed the insatiable appetite of the knowledge economy.

In the peculiar language of research policy, research that is not 'blue-sky' is classified as either 'practice-led' or 'problem-oriented'. If it is practice-led it is supposed to give rise to new things, such as works of art, architecture or design; it is creative. If it is problem-oriented it is supposed to draw on existing knowledge to devise procedures for solving problems and deliver their solutions; it is applied. You might wonder, on the one hand, what research is not practical in its implementation? Or what scholarly endeavours are not creative? And on the other hand, you might wonder whether any of the problems that we are called upon to solve actually have their solutions hidden inside. Real problems, as we saw in Chapter 3, always exceed their solutions and are never dissolved by them. It is in this excess, and not in the novelty of artefacts or answers thrown up along the way, that the genuine creativity of research is to be found. In the pursuit of truth, research is as much about the discovery of questions *in* practice as about the answering of them *by way of* practice, and the former continually overflows the latter. In short, *real* research is neither practice-led nor problem-oriented, in the sense that the practice or problem is the initiator from which everything follows; rather practices and problems engender one another, as chicken and egg, in the educational process of leading life. Nor is it even possible, in this process, to set curiosity aside from care. For at the end of the day, 'care, not impact, is the hallmark of the ethically responsible search for truth'.[37]

Anti-disciplinary interdisciplinarity

In a formulation that we owe to the philosophy of Immanuel Kant, the task of academic labour is to map the data of experience as they are revealed to the senses, in all their abundance and complexity, into the appropriate compartments of the mind, so as to render apparent their relationships, connections and mutual dispositions. The discipline, in this conception, is taken to mean a particular territory, staked out in the mind's interior architecture just as the phenomena with which it deals are staked out in the exterior architecture of the world. But what would happen if we were to rethink the concept of the discipline in the same way that we have rethought the practices of both art and science, imagining the scholar-practitioner not as one who struggles *against* the obstacles and resistances that objects of knowledge throw in his tracks, hoping for a breakthrough, but as one who works *with* things, finding their grain and bending it to his investigative purpose? What if we thought of scholarship, thus, as soft rather than hard – as an ongoing process of interstitial differentiation? The entirety of knowledge would then appear not as a continent divided into territories or *fields of study* but as a tangled mesh of ongoing pathways or *lines of interest*.

Every scholar, as Kekulé taught, is a pathfinder, improvising his line as he goes along, and following whatever clues, fragments of evidence, hunches or conjectures come his way. Sometimes, numerous paths converge, and the scholar may find himself following trails that many have trodden before, in the company of those still treading them now. But his line may just as well diverge, going off into previously unexplored thickets, or joining up with other convergences. The scholar's path, however, is a continuous one. Whatever its twists and turns, or its convergences with and divergences from other paths, it crosses no territorial boundaries. In practice, every discipline is a more or less temporary convergence: not a bounded field but a binding of lines of interest spun by its several practitioners. And since the spinning continues as practitioners proceed on their way, the discipline is both processual and open-ended. When disciplines no longer offer a way ahead they do not so much fragment as unravel, as their constituent lines drift off in other directions only to bind with other lines in other convergences. The overall tangle of lines, ravelling here and unravelling there, comprises the great tapestry of knowledge that scholarship is forever weaving.

Nonetheless there is much talk, today, of interdisciplinarity. Up to now, it is said, scholars have been walled up within disciplinary silos. They need to get out more. No doubt this is all to the good. I am troubled, however, by the connotation of the prefix *inter-*, in 'interdisciplinary'. For its effect is to emphasise the 'between-ness' of the endeavour, as though disciplines were closed domains that could be connected only by some kind of bridging operation. Such an operation is inherently detemporalising, cutting across the ways of knowing comprising the discipline rather than moving along with them. In just the same way, the concept of *inter*action cuts across paths of human movement and becoming, as the concept of *inter*national cuts across the histories of nations. In every case the *inter-*, the focus on between-ness, is complicit in setting up the very borders it is alleged to cross. Nations become territorial states, actors square up to one another in the *vis-à-vis*, and scholars find themselves on opposite sides of fences that had not been there before.

My proposal is that we should reconceive scholarly work – as indeed the histories of nations and the processes of social life – on the principle of togethering rather than othering.[38] This is to substitute for interaction a correspondence of disciplinary *agencements* moving together through time. It is to think of knowing as a becoming that runs not across and between but through and along. In practice, of course, this is how scholarship has always been done, in the midstream. Knowledge no more comes with the territory than does our own humanity; like the latter, it is something we have continually to work at. The alleged 'problem' of interdisciplinarity does not therefore arise in the ordinary course of scholarly work. It arises, rather, in the territorialisation of knowledge: in the attempt to organise what are seen as the 'results' of scholarship, its finalities, into the compartments of a total system. For the organisational system-builders, the value of interdisciplinarity lies precisely in the opportunities it affords to think holistically, in terms of the totality of joined-up knowledge.

This ambition, however, can impede scholarship in three ways. First, when interdisciplinarity itself becomes self-conscious, the open-ended pursuit of lines of inquiry takes second place to the formation and communication of closed disciplinary identities. In this, the stretch of attention in commoning gives way to the assertion of what practitioners already have in common to begin with, thanks to the transmission of disciplinary content. Second, in an architectonics of knowledge conceived as having a segmentary structure, the path from one discipline to another can only be negotiated by way of the larger blocks within which they are nested. Instead of following a multitude of interweaving pathways, communication is constrained to run along arterial routes between these blocks – such as 'natural science', 'social science', 'the arts' and 'the humanities'. And third, to think of the discipline as a compartment within an architectonic structure is to reduce it from what it really is, or should be – namely, a conversation among fellow travellers following convergent lines of interest – to a particular and regimented body of data, method and theory. In short, the project of interdisciplinarity, insofar as it runs across rather than along, and between rather than through, creates rather more barriers than it removes.

That is why my call is for a kind of disciplinarity that is, paradoxically, *anti-disciplinary*.[39] It is anti-disciplinary in that it seeks to undo, rather than reinforce, the territorialisation of knowledge – its division into bounded compartments. By appealing to an anti-disciplinary interdisciplinarity I want to celebrate the openness of knowing from the inside, as against the closures of totalisation and compartmentalisation. As noted above, this is not new – it is how scholars have always worked. Conversations among scholars of different disciplines have been going on all along, as an almost taken-for-granted background to good practice. Why, then, are calls for interdisciplinarity becoming so insistent? These calls come, by and large, not from scholars but from the managers and funders of research. It is in their heads, and theirs alone, that the notion of the discipline as a hidebound compartment of knowledge persists. It is they who insist on comparing disciplines to silos. They would like to be able to engineer interdisciplinarity, by fixing it to structures of governance and resource management. Theirs is a formula not for flexible, open-ended inquiry but for the formalisation, compartmentalisation and bureaucratisation of knowledge. Perhaps it is but a smokescreen for greater managerialism and control. If so, we should challenge it. We will do so, however, not by closing the doors on our respective disciplines, but by refuting the idea that disciplines are, or ever have been, closed to one another. They have not. Disciplines do not interact, they correspond, and to correspond their practitioners have to enter the midstream. And anthropology, par excellence, is an anti-discipline of the midstream. It depends for its vitality on the correspondences of life. Outside the current, beached and stranded, it would simply dry up.

Anthropology and the coming university

Anthropology's home has always been the university. This is not just because universities are places where the majority of professional anthropologists find employment. Anthropology and the university are joined in a more fundamental way, which lies historically in a common commitment to universality: the universality of man, and the universality of knowledge. At least since the eighteenth century, and the dawn in Europe of that great intellectual project known as the Enlightenment, the institution of the university has rested on a certain view of the uniqueness of mankind. We humans can know the world and ourselves, it was supposed, in a way no other animal can. Other animals, unable to detach themselves from the conditions of their existence in the world, can have no way of knowing things for what they are. Humans alone can transcend these conditions: they can break out of nature, see it objectively, from the outside, and see themselves as well, reflected in its mirror. Or at least, more enlightened and civilised humans can. Others, the so-called 'savage nations' that European-led voyages of exploration were discovering around the world, still appeared to bask in ignorance of their real condition, to be mired in custom and superstition, and living lives that were little better – and sometimes worse – than those of animals. Yet they too, unlike the animals, were endowed with minds of equal capacity to those of humans anywhere, and therefore – again unlike the animals – they could be educated. They could be raised from savagery to civilisation. It was the specific task of the academy to undertake this educational mission. For Enlightenment thinkers the university represented the pinnacle of civilisation, the vanguard that would pull the rest of humanity in its wake, spreading the light of learning to all nations and delivering their citizens from ignorance, poverty and subjugation.

These were noble ideals. Paternalistic and ethnocentric they may have been, but honourable nonetheless, underpinned by a commitment to the common good. Universities were progressive institutions, and their legitimate aspirations were backed by the conviction of shared human potential. And anthropology, insofar as it cleaved to the same ideals, was a progressive discipline. Yet it is undeniable that universities – and along with them, anthropology – were also responsible for inventing and enforcing the condition of savagery, not to say complicit in the very regimes of colonial oppression from which they offered release, if only for a privileged minority. Much of anthropology's twentieth-century history was caught up in the dilemmas stemming from its desire to admit all nations or cultures to the 'family of man', while continuing to serve as the handmaiden of a colonial regime that subjugated some to the benefit of others. With their tradition of long-term fieldwork, anthropologists were exposed to these dilemmas to a degree not felt by practitioners of other disciplines. Drawing on first-hand experience of real life among subaltern populations, they have been among the most vociferous agents of the post-colonial critique of 'western' modernity. For a while this critique came virtually to define the discipline, putting it at odds with an academic establishment which continued to assert in principle, and reproduce in practice, its claims to superior intelligence. Indeed, no discipline has done more than anthropology, over the past several decades, to expose the power relations that underpin traditional hierarchies of knowledge, or to question the claims of universal reason and empirical objectivity upon which they rest. In devoting so much of its energy to challenging the legitimacy of these hierarchies, and to demonstrating the force and integrity of ways of knowing rooted in diverse practices of ordinary life, anthropology has emerged as perhaps the most virulently anti-academic of academic disciplines. Chipping away at the foundations of modernity, it has seemed intent on toppling the very ivory towers in which it had once made itself comfortably at home.

Today, however, we are living through an epochal moment in the history of the university. After almost three centuries, the Enlightenment model of academic knowledge production is on the verge of collapse, if it has not already crumbled, along with the once hegemonic powers that sustained it. And as tends to happen at such moments, far from reaching an accommodation that would open up to other ways of knowing and being, and to voices previously muted or suppressed, we are witnessing just the opposite, with the emergence on all sides of closed and self-righteous fundamentalisms, whether religious, political or economic – of church, state or market. Together, these movements pose an unprecedented threat to future democracy and peaceful coexistence. Universities, however, are currently doing little to address this threat. On the contrary, the collapse of their 'top-down' civilising mission has left a vacuum that is all too readily filled by corporate interests.[40] Like many other public bodies, universities present soft targets for market-led profiteering. But there is no sign that the regimes of management which have arrogated to themselves the business of controlling what they call the 'sector' – their name for what has become a lucrative global business – have adequately grasped the issues at stake. Their myopic vision for higher education is circumscribed by crude indices of rank and productivity. Teaching is indexed by student satisfaction and employability, research by innovation and commercial potential. These criteria have nothing to do with democratic education, and everything to do with reproducing the knowledge economy, along with the disenfranchisement and inequality it inevitably brings in train. The educational mission that universities inherited from the Enlightenment now survives in name only, emblazoned on branding logos or inscribed in banal mission statements. My own institution is typical of many: its brand is 'illumination', a one-word thought with which it hopes to reach out to markets across the world. Enlightenment, it seems, is up for sale, and you can buy it here!

If universities are to pave the way for a sustainable future, then it is imperative that they redefine their purpose. Not only must education be restored to the university, but also and perhaps more importantly, the university must be restored to education. For education is not a sector – not a subdivision of the knowledge economy – but a process of leading life. It is no longer an option for universities to shelter behind self-serving appeals to academic immunity that have ceased to have any traction beyond their walls, nor can they simply surrender to the anti-democratic forces that would prefer to see them destroyed or taken over. In today's world, we need universities more than ever. We need them to bring people of all ages and from all nations together, across their multiple differences, and we need them as places where these differences can be voiced and debated in an ecumenical spirit of tolerance, justice and fellowship. No purpose is more important, and no institution, apart from the university, currently exists with the capacity to undertake it.

For no discipline other than anthropology, moreover, is this purpose already so deeply inscribed in its constitution. For anthropology's core qualities, of generosity, open-endedness, comparison and criticality are precisely those that will come to define the educational purpose of the university. Once again, as in the heyday of the Enlightenment, the fortunes of anthropology and of the university are joined at the hip. Yet as I have argued in this chapter, for anthropology to realise its true emancipatory potential it must take a step beyond ethnography, and switch from othering to togethering, so as to bring those with whom we study into presence in order that we can learn from them, debate with them and even disagree with them – just as they can learn from, debate with and disagree with us. That's the way to forge a sustainable world which has room for everyone. But this, too, is surely the way of the coming university. The future for anthropology, in short, is no less than the future for the university. It will be a future founded on the principles of *freedom* and *universality*. By way of conclusion, I shall say a few words about each.

The multiversity, one world

The question of freedom is of massive significance for education, whether in the school or the university, and indeed for democracy itself. It is a hollow freedom, however, that can be secured only by subjecting the world in which it is exercised to the governance of mechanical necessity. The consequence is inevitable, so long as freedom is defined, as it is in the discourses of the majority, by way of its opposition to predetermination. It is this opposition that leads people of Culture, whose mantra is 'freedom of expression' in fields for example art and literature, to imagine that the behaviour of other people is culturally determined, that leads scientists to imagine that indigenous folk are shackled to tradition, and that leads pedagogues to suppose that children are still in the grip of innate predispositions. In every case, freedom can be configured for some only against the ground of captivity for others. This is the freedom of volition. In its modern articulation it has taken on the character of a right, or entitlement, to be exercised by individuals – whether individually or collectively – in the defence of their interests. Applied to the university, it leads to the perception of its academics as an interest group, a scholarly elite, jealous in the protection of exclusive rights and privileges founded on a claim of intellectual superiority and denied to lesser folk who are cast as the mere beneficiaries of learning. It should come as no surprise that appeals to academic freedom couched in these terms cut little ice in a wider society suspicious of all forms of elitism and claims to higher intelligence or expertise.

In its appropriation by the modern university, however, the concept of freedom has been falsified. As we saw in Chapter 3, the true meaning of the concept lies not in what one *has* but in what one *is*. Real freedom is not a property but a mode of existence – a way of being that is fundamentally open to others and to the world rather than hemmed in by aims and objectives. Such freedom holds no promise of immunity. It offers no protection, nor any hiding place. On the contrary, it is a form of exposure. Real freedom in the academy rests on a readiness to relinquish the comfort of established positions, to take the risk of pushing out into the unknown, where outcomes are uncertain and destinations yet to be mapped.[41] This is the freedom of the undercommons. Far from founding its legitimacy on the premise of an original inequality of intelligence, real academic freedom assumes by default that all human beings are of equal intellect and, by the same token, equally free. Thus the freedom exercised by scholars cannot, in principle, be distinct from the freedom exercised by everyone else; it differs only insofar as it is an intensification of that freedom. Academic freedom is, in this sense, *exemplary*. Like citizenship, like humanity, it is not handed down on a plate but rather arrives as a task that falls to us – as a duty we owe to others. And like any task, it has to be performed. Freedom is performed, in the academy, in the activities of teaching, research and scholarship, and exemplified in the scholar's relations with peers, with students and with society at large. It is always work in progress; we can never give up on it and assume that it has been won.[42] As Dewey put it, in an essay on 'individuality and experience' published in 1926, 'freedom … is not an original possession or a gift. It is something to be achieved, to be wrought out.'[43] This is the freedom not of volition but of habit.

Finally, with such a concept of freedom, what happens to universality? The project of the Enlightenment, as we have seen, rested on the presumption that human beings are alike in their innate possession of the basic faculties of mind. This presumption crystallised in the mid-nineteenth century in the doctrine of the 'psychic unity of mankind', attributed to the German ethnologist and polymath Adolf Bastian, whence it became a founding principle of the newly developing discipline of anthropology. Axiomatically, human beings differ the world over, in manners and customs, or in what came to be called 'culture', but only thanks to a 'capacity for culture' common to all. Education, then, is understood in the strong sense, to be the process that fills this capacity with content. My argument throughout has been against this strong sense of education, and as a corollary, against the idea of a universal human essence by which our kind is allegedly set free from the determinations of nature, and raised above the rest of creation. Must we, then, give up on universality? Not at all. But we do have to cease defining the universal in terms of the prior attribution, to each and every individual, of a common essence. We all inhabit a universe, to be sure, but it is a universe not of being but becoming, not of underlying similarity but of infinite and perpetual differentiation. In this universe of becoming, though each of us may be different, these differences are constituted in and through the generative processes of life; they do not exist in spite of it. Instead of separating universality and difference on opposite sides of a division between natural and cultural, innate and acquired, we need to put them back together again. This is to acknowledge, with philosopher Alain Badiou, that 'the single world is precisely the place where an unlimited set of differences exist… Far from casting doubt on the unity of the world, these differences are its principle of existence.'[44]

What should we call it, this single world of ours? In 1908, a century before Badiou, William James – pragmatist philosopher and standard-bearer for Dewey – delivered the Hibbert Lectures at the University of Oxford, under the title *A Pluralistic Universe*.[45] Unlike the monistic universe, the pluralistic universe, or what James called the 'multiverse' for short, has no boundaries of inclusion or exclusion. Regardless of the part or element on which we choose to focus, at whatever level of exclusiveness or inclusiveness, there is always an overflow of relations. The sentences of the Jamesian world are never finished: 'nothing includes everything, or dominates over everything. The word "and" trails along after every sentence. Something always escapes.'[46] The multiverse, in short, is defined, not by what its participants have in common but by their commoning. It is in the course of education – of leading life – that this commoning is carried on. Let the coming university, then, be a place of commoning; let it be a multiversity! And let anthropology, as the beating heart of the university, be multiversal in its scope! But let us also never lose sight of the principle that the multiverse is one world nonetheless, that it is a *singular* plural,[47] bound together rather than divided by its differences. This one world, opening up in the midst of its differentiation, in all its richness and profundity, is where we study. *The one world is our multiversity.*

Notes

1 Barad (2007: 185).
2 This section draws substantially on what I have written elsewhere in Ingold (2014b).
3 Jackson (1989: 51).
4 Ingold (2013b: 5).
5 Jackson (1989: 51).
6 Burridge (1975: 10).
7 Dewey (2015: 35).
8 Jackson (2013: 28, original emphasis).
9 Jackson (2013: 88).
10 Rorty (1980: 370).
11 Masschelein (2010b: 46).
12 Jackson (2013: 28).
13 Harney and Moten (2013: 109–110).
14 Biesta (2013: 33).
15 Manning (2016: 20).
16 Manning (2016: 224).
17 Fabian (1983: 37).
18 For a like-minded criticism of rapport, as a back-handed 'technique' of intelligence gathering, see Marcus (2001).
19 Ingold (2011: 222). On the art of describing, see Alpers (1983).
20 Foster (1995: 305).
21 Foster (1995: 305).
22 Foster (1995: 303).
23 Gell (1996: 37).
24 Gell (1996: 36).
25 Kandinsky (1979: 27). Kandinsky's essay, *Punkt und Linie zu Fläche*, was first published in 1926.
26 On the influences of Siberian animism and shamanism on Kandinsky's art, see Weiss (1995).
27 Philippe Descola refers to 'description, comprehension and explanation' as the 'classical three stages of anthropological research', noting nevertheless that these operations, in practice, 'are most often intertwined' (Descola 2005: 72).
28 Radcliffe-Brown (1957).
29 Radcliffe-Brown (1952: 3).
30 Sansi (2015: 143).
31 Holdrege (2005) offers an excellent summary of the Goethean way of doing science.
32 Kekulé, in Benfey (1958: 23).
33 Ingold (2013c: 747).

34 I have drawn in this section on my responses in dialogue with Judith Winter. See Ingold and Winter (2016).
35 Lewis (2011: 592).
36 Rancière (1991: 33).
37 The phrase is taken from the *Manifesto* for 'Reclaiming our University' (RoU 2016: §19).
38 I take the 'principle of togetherness' from the work of the great Swedish geographer Torsten Hägerstrand (1976: 332).
39 Ingold (2013b: 12).
40 Much has been written on the corporatisation of higher education, and its consequences. For a recent review, from an anthropological perspective, see Shore and Wright (2015).
41 RoU (2016: §8).
42 RoU (2016: §9).
43 Dewey (1964: 156).
44 Badiou (2008: 39).
45 James (2012).
46 James (2012: 167).
47 Nancy (2000).

CODA

There, I'm done. That's my argument complete. But having set it out, I worry: have I practised what I preach? I have not shied away from taking a stand, from setting out exactly what I am *for* (attention) and *against* (transmission). I have done my best to write in coherent sentences, each beginning with an upper case letter and ending with a full stop. I have endeavoured to ensure that these sentences, and the verdicts they pronounce, are mutually consistent and joined up. And having joined them up, I declare the job finished. Yet what have I argued? That to restore the world to presence, and to allow life to carry on, we should climb down from our defensive standpoints, lay aside the weapons of adversarial combat, and answer to one another in a spirit of responsivity and care. I have argued that we should release thinking from the prison-house of sentences, allow things to unravel and celebrate loose ends – for only if there are such ends to pick up can the generations that follow us begin afresh. A book that would live up to these expectations would be like a landscape. When you walk in a landscape you may choose – for reasons of practicality or time commitment – to begin here and end there. But the landscape itself goes on and on. Some books are like that. They begin nowhere in particular, carry on for a few hundred pages, and then trail off in the midst of things, leaving innumerable loose ends for readers to follow according to their inclinations. Such books are not meant to be read from cover to cover. Yet as with taking a walk in the landscape, you have only to dip in to the text at some point and follow it for a while, and you can be sure to discover things you had not noticed before.

The book I have just finished writing is not like that. I have not set out to fabulate a landscape. I hope that you have read it from beginning to end; as books go, after all, it is not that long! But I also hope that when you next go walking in the landscape, whether terrestrial or textual, it will open up to you in ways that may give cause for curiosity and care. Perhaps you will be inspired to search, and search again. I hope, in short, that the book will open some of the doors to research that majoritarian discourses of life-leading, or of education, have firmly closed. To open doors, of course, you need a key, and this key needs to be both precisely wrought and complete in its configuration of grooves and notches. Moreover these grooves and notches must be cut in such a way that they negate, at every turn, the points embedded in the lock. In this book I have aimed to fashion such a key. Inevitably, then, it has something of the character of the lock that it unpicks. That, at any rate, is my excuse. Whether you find it compelling, or just a case of special pleading, I leave to you – the reader – to decide. I will merely close with an observation. On 15 January, 2017, I wrote the briefest of entries in my notebook: 'I finished the last chapter today!' This was the same pocket notebook in which many of the sentences in this book were forged, and – with pencil and spectacles – it forms an essential part of my writer's toolkit. Most of the sentences pencilled in the notebook are unfinished, and they are rough at the edges. And it turns out that the little note of 15 January was no final flourish. With the passage of days, it was soon overwhelmed by further scribbling as the moment of inscription faded into the distance. These scribbles will have to wait for another work. But they give me confidence that there is life beyond the book – beyond both my writing it and your reading it. I can finish writing, and you can finish reading, but life carries on. And so, thankfully, does education.

REFERENCES

Agrawal, A. 1995. 'Dismantling the divide between indigenous and scientific knowledge'. *Development and Change* 26: 413–439.

Alpers, S. 1983. *The Art of Describing: Dutch Art in the Seventeenth Century*. London: Penguin.

Arendt, H. 1958. *The Human Condition*. Chicago, IL: University of Chicago Press.

Badiou, A. 2008. 'The communist hypothesis'. *New Left Review* 49: 29–42.

Bamford, S. and J. Leach (eds) 2009. *Kinship and Beyond: The Genealogical Model Reconsidered*. Oxford: Berghahn.

Barad, K. 2007. *Meeting the Universe Halfway*. Durham, NC: Duke University Press.

Baron-Cohen, S., M. Lombardo and H. Tager-Flusberg (eds) 1993. *Understanding Other Minds: Perspectives from Developmental Social Neuroscience*. Oxford: Oxford University Press.

Benfey, O.T. 1958. 'August Kekulé and the birth of the structural theory of organic chemistry in 1858'. *Journal of Chemical Education* 35: 21–23.

Biesta, G. J. J. 2006. *Beyond Learning: Democratic Education for a Human Future*. Boulder, CO: Paradigm Publishers.

Biesta, G. J. J. 2013. *The Beautiful Risk of Education*. Boulder, CO: Paradigm Publishers.

Blackmore, S. 2000. *The Meme Machine*. Oxford: Oxford University Press.

Bloch, M. 2005. *Essays on Cultural Transmission*. Oxford: Berg.

Boesch, C. 1991. 'Teaching among wild chimpanzees'. *Animal Behavior* 41: 530–532.

Boesch, C. 2003. 'Is culture a golden barrier between human and chimpanzee?' *Evolutionary Anthropology* 12: 82–91.

Boesch, C. and M. Tomasello 1998. 'Chimpanzee and human cultures'. *Current Anthropology* 39(5): 591–614.

Bollier, D. and S. Helfrich (eds) 2015. *Patterns of Commoning*. Amherst, MA: Levellers Press.

Bourdieu, P. 1977. *Outline of a Theory of Practice*, trans. R. Nice. Cambridge, UK: Cambridge University Press.

Burridge, K. 1975. 'Other people's religions are absurd'. In *Explorations in the Anthropology of Religion: Essays in Honour of Jan van Baal*, eds. W. E. A. van Beek and J. H. Scherer. The Hague: Martinus Nijhoff, pp. 8–24.

Cage, J. 2011. *Silence: Letters and Writings*, 50th Anniversary Edition. Middletown, CT: Wesleyan University Press.

Carlisle, C. 2014. *On Habit*. Abingdon: Routledge.

Caro, T. M. and M. D. Hauser 1992. 'Is there teaching in nonhuman animals?' *The Quarterly Review of Biology* 67(2): 151–174.

Cruikshank, J. 1998. *The Social Life of Stories: Narrative and Knowledge in the Yukon Territory*. Lincoln: University of Nebraska Press.

Dawkins, R. 1976. *The Selfish Gene*. Oxford: Oxford University Press.

Deleuze, G. and F. Guattari 2004. *A Thousand Plateaus: Capitalism and Schizophrenia*, trans. B. Massumi. London: Continuum.

Descola, P. 2005. 'On anthropological knowledge'. *Social Anthropology* 13(1): 65–73.

Descola, P. 2013. *Beyond Nature and Culture*, translated by J. Lloyd. Chicago, IL: University of Chicago Press.

Desjarlais, R. 2011. *Counterplay: An Anthropologist at the Chessboard*. Berkeley, CA: University of California Press.

Dewey, J. 1964. *John Dewey on Education: Selected Writings*, ed. R. D. Archambault. Chicago, IL: University of Chicago Press.

Dewey, J. 1966. *Democracy and Education: An Introduction to the Philosophy of Education*. New York: Free Press.

Dewey, J. 1987. 'Art as experience'. In *John Dewey: The Later Works, 1925–1953, Vol. 10: 1934*, ed. J. A. Boydston. Carbondale, IL: Southern Illinois University Press.

Dewey, J. 2015. *Experience and Education*. New York: Free Press.

Durham, W. H. 1991. *Coevolution: Genes, Culture and Human Diversity*. Stanford, CA: Stanford University Press.

Eder, D. J. 2007. 'Bringing Navajo storytelling practices into schools: the importance of maintaining cultural integrity'. *Anthropology & Education Quarterly* 38(3): 278–296.

Esposito, R. 2012. *Terms of the Political: Community, Immunity, Biopolitics*, trans. R. N. Welch. New York: Fordham University Press.

Fabian, J. 1983. *Time and the Other: How Anthropology Makes its Object*. New York: Columbia University Press.

Foster, H. 1995. 'The artist as ethnographer?' In *The Traffic in Culture: Refiguring Art and Anthropology*, eds. G. E. Marcus and F. R. Myers. Berkeley, CA: University of California Press, pp. 302–309.

Gärdenfors, P. and A. Högberg 2017. 'The archaeology of teaching and the evolution of *Homo docens*'. *Current Anthropology* 58(2): 188–208.

Gell, A. 1985. 'How to read a map: remarks on the practical logic of navigation'. *Man* (N.S.) 20: 271–286.

Gell, A. 1996. 'Vogel's net: traps as artworks and artworks as traps'. *Journal of Material Culture* 1(1): 15–38.

Gibson, J. J. 1979. *The Ecological Approach to Visual Perception*. Boston: Houghton Mifflin.

Hägerstrand, T. 1976. 'Geography and the study of the interaction between nature and society'. *Geoforum* 7: 329–334.

Harney, S. and F. Moten 2013. *The Undercommons: Fugitive Planning and Black Study*. Wivenhoe: Minor Compositions.

Hatley, J. D. 2003. 'Taking phenomenology for a walk: the artworks of Hamish Fulton'. In *Lived Images: Mediations in Experience, Life-World and I-hood*, eds. M. Itkonen and G. Backhaus. Jyväskylä: University of Jyväskylä Press, pp. 194–216.

Holdrege, C. 2005. 'Doing Goethean science'. *Janus Head* 8: 27–52.

Home-Cook, G. 2015. *Theatre and Aural Attention: Stretching Ourselves*. Basingstoke: Palgrave Macmillan.

Ingold, T. 2000. *The Perception of the Environment: Essays on Livelihood, Dwelling and Skill*. London: Routledge.

Ingold, T. 2001. 'From the transmission of representations to the education of attention'. In *The Debated Mind: Evolutionary Psychology versus Ethnography*, ed. H. Whitehouse. Oxford: Berg, pp. 113–153.

Ingold, T. 2002. 'Between evolution and history: biology, culture, and the myth of human origins'. *Proceedings of the British Academy* 112: 43–66.

Ingold, T. 2005. 'Time, memory and property'. In *Property and Equality, Volume 1: Ritualisation, Sharing, Egalitarianism*, eds. T. Widlok and W. G. Tadesse. Oxford: Berghahn, pp. 165–174.

Ingold, T. 2007. *Lines: A Brief History*. Abingdon: Routledge.

Ingold, T. 2011. *Being Alive: Essays on Movement, Knowledge and Description*. Abingdon: Routledge.

Ingold, T. 2013a. 'Prospect'. In *Biosocial Becomings: Integrating Social and Biological Anthropology*, eds. T. Ingold and G. Palsson. Cambridge, UK: Cambridge University Press, pp. 1–21.

Ingold, T. 2013b. *Making: Anthropology, Archaeology, Art and Architecture*. Abingdon: Routledge.

Ingold, T. 2013c. 'Dreaming of dragons: on the imagination of real life'. *Journal of the Royal Anthropological Institute* (N.S.) 19: 734–752.

Ingold, T. 2014a. 'The creativity of undergoing'. *Pragmatics & Cognition* 22(1): 124–139.

Ingold, T. 2014b. 'That's enough about ethnography!' *HAU: Journal of Ethnographic Theory* 4(1): 383–395.

Ingold, T. 2015. *The Life of Lines*. Abingdon: Routledge.

Ingold, T. 2016a. 'A naturalist abroad in the museum of ontology: Philippe Descola's *Beyond Nature and Culture*'. *Anthropological Forum* 26(1): 301–320.

Ingold, T. 2016b. *Evolution and Social Life* (new edition). Abingdon: Routledge.

Ingold, T. and T. Kurttila 2000. 'Perceiving the environment in Finnish Lapland'. *Body and Society* 6(3–4): 183–196.

Ingold, T. and J. Winter 2016. 'Pursuing truth'. *Archis* 48: 43–48.

Jackson, M. 1989. *Paths Toward a Clearing: Radical Empiricism and Ethnographic Inquiry*. Bloomington, IN: Indiana University Press.

Jackson, M. 2013. *Essays in Existential Anthropology*. Chicago, IL: Chicago University Press.

James, W. 2012. *A Pluralistic Universe* [1909]. Auckland, NZ: The Floating Press.

Kandinsky, W. 1979. *Point and Line to Plane*, trans. H. Dearstyne and H. Rebay, ed. H. Rebay. Mineola, NY: Dover Publications.

Lave, J. 1990. 'The culture of acquisition and the practice of understanding'. In *Cultural Psychology: Essays on Comparative Human Development*, eds J. W. Stigler, R. A. Shweder and G. Herdt. Cambridge, UK: Cambridge University Press, pp. 309–327.

Lave, J. 2011. *Apprenticeship in Critical Ethnographic Practice*. Chicago, IL: University of Chicago Press.

Lave, J. and E. Wenger 1991. *Situated Learning: Legitimate Peripheral Participation*. Cambridge, UK: Cambridge University Press.

Lévi-Strauss, C. 1964. *Totemism*, trans. R. Needham. London: Merlin Press.

Lewis, D. 1975. *We, the Navigators: The Ancient Art of Landfinding in the Pacific*. Canberra: Australian National University Press.

Lewis, T. E. 2011. 'Rethinking the learning society: Giorgio Agamben on studying, stupidity, and impotence'. *Studies in Philosophy and Education* 30: 585–599.

Lingis, A. 1994. *The Community of Those Who Have Nothing in Common*. Bloomington, IN: Indiana University Press.

Lowie, R. H. 1921. *Primitive Society*. London: Routledge & Kegan Paul.

Lowie, R. H. 1937. *The History of Ethnological Theory*. London: Harrap.

Manning, E. 2016. *The Minor Gesture*. Durham, NC: Duke University Press.

Marcus, G. E. 2001. 'From rapport under erasure to theaters of complicit reflexivity'. *Qualitative Inquiry* 7(4): 519–528.

Masschelein, J. 2010a. 'The idea of critical e-ducational research – e-ducating the gaze and inviting to go walking'. In *The Possibility/Impossibility of a New Critical Language of Education*, ed. I. Gur-Ze'ev. Rotterdam: Sense Publishers, pp. 275–291.

Masschelein, J. 2010b. 'E-ducating the gaze: the idea of a poor pedagogy'. *Ethics and Education* 5(1): 43–53.

Masschelein, J. 2011. 'Experimentum scholae: the world once more … but not (yet) finished'. *Studies in Philosophy and Education* 30: 529–535.

Masschelein, J. and M. Simons 2013. *In Defence of the School: A Public Issue*, trans. J. McMartin. Leuven: E-ducation, Culture & Society Publishers.

Masschelein, J. and M. Simons. 2014. 'The university in the ears of its students: on the power, architecture and technology of university lectures'. In *Die Idee der Universität – Revisited*, ed. N. Ricken, H.-C. Koller and E. Keiner. Wiesbaden: Springer Fachmedien, pp. 173–192.

Mauss, M. 1979. 'Body techniques'. In *Sociology and Psychology: Essays*. London: Routledge and Kegan Paul, pp. 97–123.

Menzies, H. 2014. *Reclaiming the Commons for the Common Good*. Gabriola Island, BC: New Society Publishers.

Nadasdy, P. 2003. *Hunters and Bureaucrats: Power, Knowledge and Aboriginal-State Relations in the Southwest Yukon*. Vancouver: UBC Press.

Nancy, J-L. 2000. *Being Singular Plural*, trans. R. D. Richardson and A. E. O'Byrne. Stanford, CA: Stanford University Press.

Ortega y Gasset, J. 1961. *History as a System, and Other Essays Toward a Philosophy of History*. New York: W. W. Norton.

Oyama, S. 1985. *The Ontogeny of Information: Developmental Systems and Evolution*. Cambridge, UK: Cambridge University Press.

Paul, R. A. 2015. *Mixed Messages: Cultural and Genetic Inheritance in the Constitution of Human Society*. Chicago, IL: Chicago University Press.

Pennac, D. 2010. *School Blues*, trans. S. Ardizzone. London: MacLehose Press.

Plutarch 1992. 'On listening'. In *Plutarch: Essays*, trans. R. Waterfield. London: Penguin.

Polanyi, M. 1958. *Personal Knowledge: Towards a Post-Critical Philosophy*. London: Routledge & Kegan Paul.

Polanyi, M. 1966. *The Tacit Dimension*. London: Routledge & Kegan Paul.

Premack, D. and A. J. Premack 1994. 'Why animals have neither culture nor history'. In *Companion Encyclopedia of Anthropology: Humanity, Culture and Social Life*, ed. T. Ingold. London: Routledge, pp. 350–365.

Radcliffe-Brown, A. R. 1952. *Structure and Function in Primitive Society*. London: Cohen & West.

Radcliffe-Brown, A. R. 1957. *A Natural Science of Society*. New York: Free Press.

Rancière, J. 1991. *The Ignorant Schoolmaster: Five Lessons in Intellectual Emancipation*, trans. K. Ross. Stanford, CA: Stanford University Press.

Richerson, P. J. and R. Boyd 1978. 'A dual inheritance model of the human evolutionary process, I: Basic postulates and a simple model'. *Journal of Social and Biological Structures* 1: 127–154.

Richerson, P. J. and R. Boyd 2008. *Not by Genes Alone: How Culture Transformed Human Evolution*. Chicago, IL: Chicago University Press.

Rivers, W. H. R. 1968. 'The genealogical method of anthropological inquiry'. In *Kinship and Social Organization*, by W. H. R. Rivers. London: Athlone Press.

Rogoff, B. 1990. *Apprenticeship in Thinking: Cognitive Development in Social Context*. New York: Oxford University Press.

Rogoff, B. 2003. *The Cultural Nature of Human Development*. New York: Oxford University Press.

Rorty, R. 1980. *Philosophy and the Mirror of Nature*. Princeton, NJ: Princeton University Press.

RoU 2016. *Reclaiming our University: The Manifesto*. https://reclaimingouruniversity.files.wordpress.com/2016/10/reclaiming-manifestofinal.pdf. Accessed 17 February 2017.

Sansi, R. 2015. *Art, Anthropology and the Gift*. London: Bloomsbury Academic.

Schütz, A. 1962. *The Problem of Social Reality* (collected papers I, ed. M. Natanson). The Hague: Nijhoff.

Serres, M. 1997. *The Troubadour of Knowledge*, trans. S. F. Glaser and W. Paulson. Ann Arbor, MI: University of Michigan Press.

Shore, C. and S. Wright 2015. 'Audit culture revisited: rankings, ratings and the reassembling of society'. *Current Anthropology* 56(3): 421–444.

Sperber, D. 1996. *Explaining Culture. A Naturalistic Approach*. Oxford: Blackwell.

Stout, D. 2005. 'The social and cultural context of stone-knapping and skill acquisition'. In *Stone Knapping: The Necessary Conditions for a Uniquely Hominin Behaviour*, eds. V. Roux and B. Bril. Cambridge: McDonald Institute for Archaeological Research, pp. 331–340.

Turnbull, D. 1991. *Mapping the World in the Mind: An Investigation of the Unwritten Knowledge of the Micronesian Navigators*. Geelong: Deakin University Press.

Tylor, E. B. 1871. *Primitive Culture* (2 vols.). London: John Murray.

Vergunst, J. L. 2008. 'Taking a trip and taking care in everyday life'. In *Ways of Walking: Ethnography and Practice on Foot*, eds. T. Ingold and J. Lee Vergunst. Aldershot: Ashgate, pp. 105–121.

Vygotsky, L. 1978. *Mind in Society: The Development of Higher Psychological Processes*. Cambridge, MA: Harvard University Press.

Wagner, R. 2016. *The Invention of Culture* (second edition). Chicago, IL: Chicago University Press.

Weiss, P. 1995. *Kandinsky and Old Russia: The Artist as Ethnographer and Shaman*. New Haven, CT: Yale University Press.

Wieman, H. N. 1961. *Intellectual Foundation of Faith*. London: Vision Press.

INDEX